The
Word and Eucharist
Handbook

Lawrence J. Johnson

Resource Publications, Inc.
San Jose, California

Editorial director: Kenneth Guentert
Managing editor: Elizabeth J. Asborno
Cover design and production: Huey Lee

Reprint Department
Resource Publications, Inc.
160 E. Virginia Street #290
San Jose, CA 95112-5876

Library of Congress Cataloging in Publication Data
Johnson, Lawrence J., 1933-
  The Word and Eucharist handbook / Lawrence J. Johnson. — Rev. ed.
   p.   cm.
  Includes bibliographical references.
  ISBN 0-89390-276-4 : $11.95
  1. Mass — Celebration — Handbooks, manuals, etc. I. Title.
BX2230.2.J64 1993
264'.3 — dc20   86-60896

97 96 95 94 93 | 5 4 3 2 1

Acknowledgment is extended for granting permission to reprint the following copyrighted material:

Excerpts from the English translation of the Introduction from *Lectionary for Mass* (second *edition typica*) © 1981, International Committee on English in the Liturgy, Inc. (ICEL); excerpts from the English translation of "Constitution on the Liturgy," "Instruction on Worship of the Eucharist," "Third Instruction on the Orderly Carrying Out of the Constitution on the Liturgy," "General Instruction of the Roman Missal," and "Directory for Masses with Children" from *Documents on the Liturgy 1963-1979: Conciliar, Papal, and Curial Texts* © 1982, ICEL. All rights reserved.

Excerpts from the *Appendix to the* General Instruction *for Dioceses of the United States of America* © 1969 and *Environment and Art in Catholic Worship* © 1978, USCC Publications Office. All rights reserved.

Contents

3. LITURGY OF THE EUCHARIST

4. CONCLUDING RITES

Preface

Central to the life of a parish is its Sunday liturgical assembly. Gathered together as Christ's body, the members of the community share a common purpose: they acknowledge the Lord present in their midst; they encounter and respond to God's Word; they offer to the Father a living sacrifice of praise which finds its deepest fulfillment in the sharing of the eucharistic meal. This celebration of Word and Eucharist is, of course, to be one of prayer — for without hearts uplifted to the Father there can be no Christian liturgy. And yet there are other, no less important, dimensions to our communal worship.

Those who participate in the Sunday assembly enter into a ritual action that embraces a vast ensemble of symbol, gesture, song, word, silence, movement, light, and color, which, in their ebb and flow, combine to say that something important is now happening in the lives of these people. Ritual elements, however, do not stand isolated from one another. There is an interaction of components. Space, for example, relates to action; gesture to word; silence to sound; music to speech.

Although it is the whole community which celebrates the liturgy, certain of its members are called upon to assume particular roles of service within the celebration. Here again, there exists an interrelatedness. The skills of one minister either enhance or weaken those of other ministers. For example, poor proclamation of the Word begets poor homilies; vapid presidential style engenders contagious boredom; poor music elicits a spiritless response. Doing worship well requires a shared reverence toward ritual, toward all who celebrate the ritual action, and toward the basic liturgical structures which unify what we do together.

Liturgy needs structures or patterns of action. These provide continuity, a sense of the familiar, a unifying bond. These patterns help avoid the uncertainties of the haphazard and the variations of personal whim. Yet there exists today the danger of what might be called "neo-rubricism," i.e., the tendency to focus on the rubric or directive so as to lose sight of meaning, intent and spirit. Liturgical historians, having well documented this phenomenon in the past, can readily predict its future: meaning subsumed by ceremonial, symbol replaced by commentary, ritual numbed by ritualism. To carry out any directive without attention to its purpose betrays a servile attitude unworthy of Christian celebration.

There is, however, another danger lurking about today. Fr. Robert Hovda pointed it out when he wrote that the clergy (and, we might add, other ministers as well) "should stop trying to do little jazzy things that they consider helpful at this or that point in any rite until they have time to stop and look at the whole rite's structure and flow" (*Living Worship*, August-September 1977). The liturgical structure for the celebration of Mass is contained in that part of the Sacramentary (Missal) called the *Order of Mass*. Together with its various explanatory documents the *Order of Mass* provides the support structure and point of departure for every community's celebration of Word and Eucharist. If the Sunday celebration in many communities still leaves much to be desired, one reason might be that ministers and planners fail to have recourse to the basic sources describing the manner in which the liturgy is to be celebrated. Skills presume knowledge. Good intentions supply for neither.

This book is designed to aid ministers and planners in acquiring a basic understanding of the structure and meaning of the *Order of Mass*. Pertinent quotations from the *General Instruction of the Roman Missal*, the official commentary explaining the celebration, are reproduced for each structural element of the Mass. Since the *Instruction* first gives a general description of the individual parts of the Mass (Chapter II) and subsequently explains the various forms of the celebration (e.g., with a congregation [Chapter IV]), as a rule only that section of the document which is most informative is quoted. And yet, at times, parallel texts from both sections of the *Instruction* are reproduced for purposes of comparison. Selections from or references to the *Introduction to the Lectionary for Mass*, the *Directory for Masses with Children*, and other pertinent documents are also provided.

A more extensive documentation may be found in *The Mystery of Faith: A Study of the Structural Elements of the Mass* (Washington, D.C.: Federation of Diocesan Liturgical Commissions). Since the church's liturgy has roots in the past, brief historical notes are often given. In addition, numerous practical suggestions for ministers and planners are included. Those willing to deepen their understanding of the Mass may profit from the numerous books and articles cited throughout the text.

A word of caution! As previously noted, the celebration of the liturgy is not a sequence of individual and isolated parts. Nor is it a series of recited texts. Liturgy is "doing" together. It is an action that embraces primary and secondary moments which themselves coalesce into major and minor patterns. Although printed guides to the Mass customarily follow the sequence of liturgical elements as found in the ritual books, it is, in the last analysis, the flow, pace, and overall contour of the celebration which the assembly experiences. This experience is paramount and must always be kept in mind by the users of this study book.

Although this book would not have been written without the assistance of many persons, I would be remiss in not explicitly acknowledging two of them: Rev. Richard A. Reissmann, chairman of the Liturgical Commission in the Diocese of Wilmington, Delaware, who contributed in many ways to the early development of the work; and Marlene Winter-Johnson, who not only offered unflagging support but also carefully read and helped edit the text.

1.

IMMEDIATE PREPARATION AND INTRODUCTORY RITES

Immediate Preparation

Overview

Gathering the Full Body of Christ. The Sunday assembly is meant to bring together the totality of the parish. No member of the community is to be excluded from the gathering. Many parishes respond to this imperative by appointing certain of its members to provide transportation to those who could not otherwise get to church.

Arrival Time. Ministers should assemble at an appointed time before the liturgy begins. This allows an opportunity for all to acquaint themselves with any unanticipated changes in the celebration as well as to attend to the physical preparation for the liturgy, e.g., checking sound equipment, insuring correct ribbon placements in the Lectionary and Sacramentary. Yet last minute rearrangement of chairs, music stands, and the like is often a sign of an ill-prepared celebration. In some communities the ministers gather for a short period of reflection in preparation for the liturgy.

Furniture and Objects. The altar, upon which lies an altar cloth, is prepared only at the beginning of the Liturgy of the Eucharist. Before the celebration the bread and wine are placed on a table from which they will later be taken for the procession with the gifts. Water, communion vessels, purificator, towel, basin for the washing of the hands, and corporal are placed at a convenient location in the altar area. The altar, it must be remembered, "is never to be used as a table of convenience or as a resting place for papers, notes, cruets, or anything else" (*Environment and Art in Catholic Worship*, 71). Being symbols in themselves, the altar and ambo (lectern) should not be utilized as signboards upon which to hang banners, slogans, etc. The altar and ambo, however, may at times be decorated with a covering, but this should never obscure the intrinsic beauty and design of these furnishings.

Floor-standing candlesticks, whose arrangement might be varied according to the occasion, are generally preferable to candles placed upon the altar. At least two candles are to be lighted. Four, six, or, if the bishop presides, seven candles may be lighted. Care should be taken as to the manner of lighting the candles. A taper, not a match, should be used for this purpose. Flowers and other similar decorations, never of artificial construction, may be arranged in the altar area and throughout the building. Yet these should never overwhelm the ritual space or constrict ritual movement.

> While it is permissible for the cross to rest on the
> altar, it is preferable that it be elsewhere...so that...
> the altar is used only for the bread and wine and
> book (*Environment and Art in Catholic Worship*, 88).

Sacramentary, Lectionary, and Other Printed Aids. Before the celebration the Sacramentary is placed near the presider's chair, never on the altar. The Book of the Gospels or the Lectionary is carried in the entrance procession by a reader. Worn and tattered ritual books are unworthy of Christian celebration. Ritual books should be "of a large (public, noble) size, good paper, strong design, handsome typography and binding" (*Environment and Art in Catholic Worship*, 91). In choosing printed participation aids for the people, communities need consider not only content but also the overall attractiveness of these books or booklets. If cheap-looking books are unsuitable for the presider and reader, they are also inappropriate for the assembly.

Welcoming the People. The assembly is to be a gathering of faith-filled people who hospitably welcome one another in Christ. This experience of "belonging" is facilitated by greeters or ushers, i.e., those men and women who have the ability to make people feel at home. When these ministers extend a friendly "good morning" and a warm handshake, they greatly contribute toward creating a feeling of welcome and hospitality. Among their other areas of service are introducing people (especially strangers or visitors) to one another, gently encouraging people to sit together, and distributing any materials needed for participation in the celebration.

Setting the Mood. Music, starting as the people begin to assemble, often helps create an atmosphere and presence leading to the celebration.

Preparing the Music. At an appropriate time shortly before the celebration begins, the cantor or leader of song rehearses any unfamiliar music with the people, e.g., psalm antiphons, new hymns, etc. Such preparation is important if the assembly is to feel comfortable with the music and thus pray better through song. The place for the cantor or leader of song is in front of the assembly, at a secondary stand, not at the ambo or pulpit. A minimum of intervention should be the hallmark of the person leading the preparation of the music. The advice of D. Julien is worth remembering.

> When a sentence will do, don't make a speech.
> When a word will do, don't use a sentence.
> When a gesture will do, don't use a word.
> When a look will do, don't use a gesture.
> (Quoted by Deiss, *Spirit and Song of the New Liturgy*, 54.)

Such warm-ups should not only be brief but should end at a determined time. Celebrations which habitually start late merely encourage late-comers.

Announcing the Theme? In many parishes it has become customary to introduce the liturgy by saying, "The theme of today's celebration is...." Yet the "theme" of every eucharistic celebration is praise and thanksgiving offered to the Father by the Son in the Holy Spirit. The motive for why the assembly has gathered for this purpose is given particular focus by the feast, season, and especially by the scriptural readings appointed for the day. Thus, at times, an introduction highlighting one of the scriptural images or motifs might be advantageous. On many occasions, however, such an introduction is superfluous. The preferred time for such a statement, if necessary, is after the presider's greeting during the introductory rites. In every case, this should be done in as concise a manner as possible.

Announcing the Entrance Song. A few moments of silent reflection before announcing the entrance song serve as an excellent transition to the liturgy.

Special attention should be given to the manner of announcing the song. One procedure is to ask the people to stand. Only when all are ready and attentive is the song announced. It is better to give the title with either the page or the number. Announcing both page and number often confuses. The use of a song-board, however, eliminates the need to give this and similar directions. In either case, instrumentalists need allow ample time so that all have sufficient opportunity to locate the song in the hymnal or other participation aid before the singing begins.

If a text has been selected to highlight a particular motif, it might, on occasion, be helpful to preface the announcement with a very short sentence indicating the connection between the particular focus of the celebration and the song. The entrance song, it must be remembered, is not a "greeting" of the presiding priest and other ministers.

In some parishes all are invited to face the main doors of the church and thus be able to see the procession as it enters.

Introductory Rites

Overview

General Instruction of the Roman Missal

24. The parts preceding the Liturgy of the Word, namely, the entrance song, greeting, penitential rite, *Kyrie*, *Gloria*, and opening prayer or collect, have the character of a beginning, introduction, and preparation.

   The purpose of these rites is that the faithful coming together take on the form of a community and prepare themselves to listen to God's Word and celebrate the Eucharist properly.

History. It was only gradually that the Mass began to include various rites preparatory to the proclamation of the Scriptures. In the West, such rites, differing according to various regions, underwent several stages of development till by the early Middle Ages they incorporated a large variety of prayers (often those of the priest and ministers alone) and ceremonies. To some extent these have been reduced by the *Order of Mass*.

Purpose. The introductory rites are to help those assembled become a celebrating community. They serve as a "call to worship" whose purpose is to create an experience of togetherness in faith as well as to prepare the assembly to hear God's Word and to celebrate the Eucharist.

Structure. The introductory rites consist of:

   Procession and song

   Sign of the Cross

   Greeting

   Introduction to the liturgy

Penitential Rite/Kyrie

Glory to God

Opening Prayer

The procession and song together with the opening prayer are considered the principal elements.

A Word of Caution. Liturgical writers often remark that the various introductory rites are not only quite numerous but also disjointed in content. What is to be a period of preparation is often cumbersome, drawn out, and uncohesive. Thus liturgy planners, musicians, and presiders need be aware that this preparatory time is of secondary importance and should be celebrated in such a way that, proper balance being maintained, the assembly is quickly led to the Liturgy of the Word. Major elements should appear as such: all else should appear as secondary. It is a question of symmetry both within the rites themselves and in the relationship of these introductory moments to the whole celebration. Verbosity, as always, must be avoided.

Masses with Children. Liturgy planners may simplify and creatively adapt the introductory rites. However,

> there should always be at least some introductory
> element, which is completed by the opening prayer.
> In choosing individual elements, care should be taken
> that each one be used from time to time and that
> none be entirely neglected (*Directory for Masses with
> Children*, 40).

Recommended Reading

Bishops' Committee on the Liturgy. *Music in Catholic Worship*, 44. Washington, D.C.: 1983.

Federation of Diocesan Liturgical Commissions. *The Mystery of Faith.* Washington, D.C.: FDLC, 1981.

Henchal, Michael J. *Sunday Worship in Your Parish.* West Mystic, Connecticut: Twenty-Third Publications, 1980.

Huck, Gabe, ed. *Liturgy with Style and Grace*. Chicago: Liturgy Training Publications, 1984.

Keifer, Ralph. "Making the Gathered Assembly a Worshipping Community." *Pastoral Music* 1, no. 4 (April-May 1977): 21-24. Reprinted in *Music in Catholic Worship: The NPM Commentary*. Ed. by Virgil C. Funk. Washington, D.C.: National Association of Pastoral Musicians, 1982.

————. "Our Cluttered Vestibule: The Unreformed Entrance Rite." *Worship* 48, no. 5 (May 1974): 270- 277.

————. *To Give Thanks and Praise*. Washington, D.C.: National Association of Pastoral Musicians, 1980.

Smolarski, Dennis C., SJ. "The Introductory Rites: A Reappraisal." *Modern Liturgy* 18, no. 6 (August 1991).

Procession and Song

General Instruction of the Roman Missal

25. After the people have assembled, the entrance song begins as the priest and the ministers come in. The purpose of this song is to open the celebration, intensify the unity of the gathered people, lead their thoughts to the mystery of the season or feast, and accompany the procession of priest and ministers.

26. The entrance song is sung alternately either by the choir and the congregation or by the cantor and the congregation; or it is sung entirely by the congregation or by the choir alone. The antiphon and psalm of the *Graduale Romanum* or *The Simple Gradual* may be used, or another song that is suited to this part of the Mass, the day, or the seasons and that has a text approved by the conference of bishops.

If there is no singing for the entrance, the antiphon in the Missal is recited either by the faithful, by some of them, or by a reader; otherwise it is recited by the priest after the greeting.

82. Once the congregation has gathered, the priest and the ministers, clad in their vestments, go to the altar in this order:

8

a)a server with a lighted censer, if incense is used;

b) the servers, who, according to the occasion, carry lighted candles and between them the crossbearer, if the cross is to be carried;

c) acolytes and other ministers;

d) a reader, who may carry the Book of the Gospels;

e) the priest who is to celebrate the Mass.

If incense is used, the priest puts some in the censer before the procession begins.

83. During the procession to the altar the entrance song is sung (see nos. 25-26).

Procession

Purpose. The formal entrance of the priest and other ministers not only serves a functional purpose, but also symbolizes that a community has come together, is beginning an action expressive of its faith-life, and is entering into God's special presence in an attitude of prayer. Moreover, the procession gives a definitive beginning to the liturgical action.

Who Should Take Part? Obviously the presiding priest. But also other ministers as the cross bearer, censer bearer, reader(s), acolytes, communion ministers, deacon, concelebrating priests, etc.

The size and solemnity of the procession should correspond to the character of the celebration. For example, on special occasions, banners, traditional in liturgical processions (e.g., Corpus Christi), add a special note of color and festivity.

Attention is to be given to the placement of the participants. Since great variety is possible, advance planning is necessary. It is important to allot adequate space between the participants so that all ministers and symbols can be easily seen.

If incense is to be used, it is placed in the censer before the procession begins.

Honor Befitting the Word of God. The rubrics say that a reader may carry the Book of the Gospels. When the Gospel Book is carried in the procession by a reader (or at times by a deacon), the Lectionary should be placed on the ambo before the celebration. The book carried in the procession should be held in a prominent fashion so that the importance of God's Word is visibly communicated. The person bearing the book should not simultaneously attempt to carry any participation aid.

The Book of the Gospels or the Lectionary, being symbols of God's Word, might be given an attractively decorated cover which could be changed according to the feasts and seasons of the liturgical year.

When to Begin. The ministers enter the assembly only after the singing begins, not during any instrumental introduction. All proceed to the altar area at a dignified pace.

Entrance Song

Purpose. The entrance song has many purposes. Its origin was functional, e.g., a chant sung by the schola to accompany the "walking in" of the ministers. Although it still fulfills this purpose, it also serves other and more important ends. Common song deepens the unity of the assembly. In fact, participation in the entrance song is the first joint endeavor of the people in the celebration. It is their first common action of service to one another. Furthermore, the very act of singing contributes toward an atmosphere of celebration, of festivity. Thus the song often highlights the feast, season, or special nature of the gathering. In brief, the entrance song unifies people and ministers as they gather to celebrate on a particular occasion.

How Long? Emphasizing its role as accompanying a procession and calling attention to the already lengthy structure of the preparation rites, some suggest that the song last only as long as is necessary to accompany the procession. Others suggest that the song continue only as long as it "takes the community to assemble itself and spiritually acclaim Christ. If only one stanza is needed, then only one stanza should be sung. If five or six stanzas are needed, the five or six should be sung..." (Deiss, *Spirit and Song of the New Liturgy*, 127). Today, however, we are often reminded of the structural unity of the majority of hymn texts. To shorten them weakens, if not at times destroys, their thematic development. And yet when a long text is sung, care should be taken not to prolong unduly the other elements in the introductory rites.

By Whom. The entrance song ordinarily involves the whole assembly. The choir can contribute to the music's impact by supplying a descant to one or more of a hymn tune's verses. The choir might also harmonize one or the other verse. When psalm texts are utilized, having the verses sung by the choir rather than by a cantor gives greater impact and festivity to the music. On some occasions short instrumental interludes between verses of psalms or hymns may be effective.

Another Element? The practice of using one piece of music (e.g., sung by the choir or performed by an instrument) to accompany the procession and then having the people sing a hymn not only does violence to the liturgical structure but also adds another element to the already lengthy introductory rites.

Selection of Music. Motifs of praise, thanksgiving, worship, joy, and gathering are always appropriate for the entrance song. The same is true for seasonal and feastday themes. Music planners should not overlook the processional psalms as especially suitable. Some hymnals and service books contain thematic indexes which are most helpful in the selection of music.

Musical Continuity. Pastoral musicians should avoid unnecessary musical "gaps" in the liturgy, especially after the entrance song. If for some reason the musical text has been completed before the presider reaches the presidential chair, e.g., because of an incensation of the altar, the organist or other instrumentalists should continue playing till he does so.

Recommended Reading

Bishops' Committee on the Liturgy. *Music in Catholic Worship*, 61. Washington, D.C.: USCC, 1983.

Crichton, J. D. *Christian Celebration: The Mass*. London: Geoffrey Chapman, 1971.

Deiss, Lucien. *Spirit and Song of the New Liturgy*. Cincinnati: World Library of Sacred Music, 1976.

Emminghaus, Johannes H. *The Eucharist: Essence, Form, Celebration*. Collegeville, Minnesota: The Liturgical Press, 1978.

Federation of Diocesan Liturgical Commissions. *The Mystery of Faith*. Washington, D.C.: FDLC, 1981.

Gelineau, Joseph. *Learning to Celebrate*. Washington, D.C.: The Pastoral Press, 1985.

National Conference of Catholic Bishops. "Appendix to the *General Instruction* for the Dioceses of the United States of America," 26.

Walsh, Eugene. *Guidelines for Effective Worship*. Phoenix: North American Liturgical Resources, 1974.

Arrival in the Altar Area

General Instruction of the Roman Missal

84. On reaching the altar the priest and ministers make a proper reverence, that is a low bow or, if there is a tabernacle containing the blessed sacrament, a genuflection.

If the cross has been carried in the procession, it is placed near the altar or at some other convenient place; the candles carried by the servers are placed near the altar or on a side table; the Book of the Gospels is placed on the altar.

85. The priest goes up to the altar and kisses it. If incense is used, he incenses the altar while circling it.

Signs of Reverence. Arriving in the altar area, the participants in the procession genuflect if the reserved Eucharist is present. (However, the Eucharist is ideally reserved in a space apart from the altar area. Refer to *Environment and Art in Catholic Worship*,

78.) If the reserved Eucharist is not present, all make a bow of the body toward the altar. The precise manner of carrying out this gesture of respect should be determined and even practiced beforehand.

Only the presider, deacon, and concelebrants kiss the altar, the symbol of Christ and his community. In cases of concelebration the details of this reverence (e.g., all together or one at a time; hands folded or placed upon the altar) should be agreed upon in advance to avoid hesitancy and lack of uniformity.

Location of Ministers. The presider and the deacon proceed to the presidential chair where the deacon assists the priest as necessary.

In many communities, readers and communion ministers are seated among the members of the assembly and only go to the altar area when they are to exercise their respective ministries. This not only avoids a proliferation of ministers in the sanctuary, but is also a sign that particular ministries are rooted in the common ministry of the whole assembly.

The cross bearer, censer bearer, acolytes, and other ministers go to their assigned places, possibly also among the assembly. If a cross is already in the sanctuary, the processional cross is placed elsewhere till the end of the celebration. This avoids a duplication of signs. The candles, placed near the altar or even on a side table if other candles are already near or on the altar, "must not interfere with the faithful's clear view of what goes on at the altar or is placed on it" (*General Instruction*, 269).

Placement of the Book. The Book of the Gospels or, in its absence, the Lectionary is placed upon the altar to symbolize the intimate relationship existing between Word and Eucharist. If the deacon is carrying the book, he first places it upon the altar and then kisses the altar with the priest.

Incensation. Incense is a sign both of honor and of the assembly's prayers ascending into heaven. Especially on more solemn occasions it is fitting for the priest, assisted by the deacon, to incense the altar and the cross. If the cross is beside the altar, the priest incenses the cross first. If it is behind the altar, he incenses the cross when he passes in front of it.

Sign of the Cross, Greeting, Introduction

General Instruction of the Roman Missal

86. The priest then goes to the chair. After the entrance song, and with all standing, the priest and the faithful make the sign of the cross. The priest says: *In the name of the Father, and of the Son, and of the Holy Spirit*; the people answer: *Amen.*

Then, facing the people and with hands outstretched, the priest greets all present, using one of the formularies indicated. He or some other qualified minister may give the faithful a very brief introduction to the Mass of the day.

Sign of the Cross

Meaning. The sign of the cross not only invokes the Trinity but also reminds the members of the assembly that they worship together as a people baptized in the name of the Father, Son, and Holy Spirit.

Some Practicalities. The priest celebrant hands his hymnal or participation aid to another minister, waits till the people have put down their books, gains the attention of all, and then makes the sign of the cross with reverence, deliberateness, and without haste. Since it is the entrance procession and song which begin the liturgy, it is incorrect to say, "Let us begin today's celebration in the name of the Father...."

Visual Focal Points. The attention of all the ministers should visually focus upon the priest when he is speaking. The same is true when a reader is proclaiming a reading or when the cantor is singing a psalm verse.

Greeting

Three Options. Option one ("The grace of our Lord Jesus Christ...") is the conclusion of St. Paul's Second Letter to the Corinthians (13:13). Option two ("The grace and peace of God our Father...") often begins certain Pauline letters, e.g., Galatians 1:3. The third option ("The Lord be with you"), having its origin in Ruth 2:4, has long been traditional in the Roman Church for recognizing the Lord amidst the gathered community. The greeting is a wish expressing and acknowledging the reality of Christ's presence among his people when they come together for prayer.

Feeling in the Words. The greeting should be joyful in tone, conveying cordiality and warmth. Eye contact is important. Greetings read from a book simply lack sincerity. The extension of the hands either accompanies or precedes the spoken words. Rapid or timid gestures contribute little to communication between presider and people. The gesture here is one of greeting: it is meant to convey something other then a gesture accompanying a prayer addressed to the Father or an invitation to prayer.

To Sing or Not to Sing. The Appendix to the Sacramentary contains various musical settings for the greeting. Singing, it may be argued, serves to unify and give strength to the dialogue. And yet we do not customarily sing greetings to one another.

Recommended Reading

Bishops' Committee on the Liturgy. "Notes on the Eucharistic Celebration: Greetings, Admonitions, Acclamations, and Responses." *Newsletter* 7, no. 12 (December 1971).

Deiss, Lucien. *Spirit and Song of the New Liturgy*. Cincinnati: World Library of Sacred Music, 1976.

Emminghaus, Johannes H. *The Eucharist: Essence, Form, Celebration*. Collegeville, Minnesota: The Liturgical Press, 1978.

Federation of Diocesan Liturgical Commissions. *The Mystery of Faith*. Washington, D.C.: FDLC, 1981.

Introduction to the Liturgy

Concrete Brevity. The presider or another minister may say a few words focusing on the particular character or tone of the celebration. Avoid sermonettes, explanations, and verbosity. If it is absolutely necessary to use printed notes, these should be placed in an attractive folder or notebook.

An Informal Greeting? Some priests use this time for an informal greeting to those assembled. Yet, such an element not only adds to an already extended liturgical structure but also seems to deny the effectiveness of the preceding ritual greeting.

Breaking Down the Walls. Some communities have inaugurated the custom of asking the people to introduce themselves to those standing nearby. Although such a practice is a small yet helpful contribution toward breaking down the feeling of anonymity and isolation characteristic of many larger assemblies, it might more fittingly take place before the celebration.

Penitential Rite

General Instruction of the Roman Missal

29. Then the priest invites them to take part in the penitential rite, which the entire community carries out through a communal confession and which the priest's absolution brings to an end.

History. Until recent years, the Roman liturgy, in contrast to those of the East, never knew a public penitential rite within the Mass. The Confiteor among the "prayers at the foot of the altar" was really the private devotion of the priest and the ministers.

During the post-Vatican II revision of the Mass, several questions arose concerning a public penitential rite. Should it even appear among the elements of the Mass? If so, should it be optional or required only for certain liturgical seasons? What should be its location? These questions were resolved by placing a simple penitential rite, with three options, among the introductory rites.

Meaning. The rite is neither a listing of sins nor an examination of conscience. Rather, it focuses on the all-embracing mercy of God whose loving forgiveness is ever at work among his people.

The Admonition. The rite begins with an admonition of the priest addressed to the people. The formula given in the Sacramentary is a model which may and should be adapted to the particular celebration or to the varying circumstances of the community.

Silence. A period of silence follows the admonition. As at other moments of silence during the celebration, it is important that adequate time be allowed. If something is to happen in the hearts and minds of the people during this time, then more than a ten second pause is imperative.

The Plea for Forgiveness. The silence leads to a plea for forgiveness. This may assume one of three forms: a more concise version of the traditional Confiteor (surprisingly enough, the only option acknowledging the horizontal dimensions of sin and forgiveness); a short invocation addressed to Christ and integrating a single "Lord, have mercy"; or a longer litany-like invocation addressed to Christ but integrating the full threefold structure of the Kyrie.

The Prayer. The rite concludes with a prayer for forgiveness.

Creativity. The Sacramentary includes eight models for the third option. These are to serve as examples for creativity in this area. In composing invocations, the liturgy planning group should follow the norms established by the Bishops' Committee on the Liturgy.

> 1. The invocations are addressed to Christ and not to the Father, Holy Spirit, Mary, or a particular saint.
>
> 2. The invocations should be brief and direct.

17

3. The content of the invocations is Christological, adaptable to the season, the feast, or the gospel reading of the day.

4. The penitential rite does not replace in style or content the general intercessions (prayer of the faithful) which have a distinct purpose.

5. Although it is suitable for the invocations to refer to the reconciling mission of Jesus, his calls to repentance of life, the forgiveness of sins, and similar concepts related to the penitential rite, they should not be turned into a kind of confession of sins or examination of conscience. In other words, the invocations are not intended — as the original model in the *Order of Mass* shows — as petitions for forgiveness but as invocations in praise of the Lord Jesus.

The use of images found in the readings serves to link the penitential rite to the Liturgy of the Word.

If the minister, who need not be the presider, is to read these invocations, they should be placed in a notebook or folder.

Singing. During a penitential season the entrance procession might be accompanied by instrumental music, and the penitential rite could be sung, especially if option two or three is used. Numerous creative possibilities exist. The priest or another minister could recite the invocation with a cantor singing the "Lord, have mercy," which is repeated by all. Or the cantor could sing both the invocations and the "Lord, have mercy" with the people repeating the latter. Music for the penitential rite is included in the Sacramentary. Some hymnals (such as *Worship*) contain many musical possibilities for judiciously enriching this rite on certain occasions. Yet the decision to sing the penitential rite must always be made in light of the balance and character of the whole celebration.

Sprinkling Rite. As an alternative to the regular options for the penitential rite, the blessing and sprinkling of holy water may take place at all Sunday Masses. The sprinkling expresses the paschal character of Sunday and is a reminder of the baptismal washing whereby we die to sin and rise unto new life with Christ.

After the presider invites the people to pray, a period of silence follows. Then a prayer of blessing is offered: one version for use during the Easter season and two others for the other Sundays of the year. Where customary, salt, a symbol of preservation and purity, is added to the water. Then the minister sprinkles himself, the other ministers, and the rest of the assembly. All should actually "feel" the water. Meanwhile an antiphon or other appropriate song is sung. Only if the Gloria follows does the presider pray the concluding formula. Otherwise, the opening prayer of the Mass immediately follows.

The music accompanying the sprinkling might be an English setting of the traditional plainsong melody for the Rite of Sprinkling (e.g., as found in *Worship*, no. 270. A hymn whose motif is baptism, cleansing, water, renewal, etc. would also be suitable. In some instances the first verses of the hymn might be used for the entrance procession, and the remaining verses could serve to accompany the sprinkling. Music planners should also consider the use of Psalm 42 (41) as being equally appropriate at this time. In any case, the music selected should not unduly prolong the rite. If the priest has not returned to the presidential chair before the end of the singing, the instrumental music should continue until he does so.

Recommended Reading

Bishops' Committee on the Liturgy. *Music in Catholic Worship*, 65. Washington, D.C.: USCC, 1983.

——. "Penitential Rite: Form Three." *Newsletter* 10 (June-July 1974): 6-7.

——. "Sunday Renewal of Baptism." *Newsletter* 8 (September-October 1972): 9-10.

Crichton, J. D. *Christian Celebration: The Mass*. London: Geoffrey Chapman, 1971.

Deiss, Lucien. *Spirit and Song of the New Liturgy*. Cincinnati: World Library of Sacred Music, 1976.

Emminghaus, Johannes H. *The Eucharist: Essence, Form, Celebration*. Collegeville, Minnesota: The Liturgical Press, 1978.

Federation of Diocesan Liturgical Commissions. *The Mystery of Faith*. Washington, D.C.: FDLC, 1981.

Gelineau, Joseph. *Learning to Celebrate*. Washington, D.C.: The Pastoral Press, 1985.

Kyrie

General Instruction of the Roman Missal

30. Then the *Kyrie* begins, unless it has already been included as part of the penitential rite. Since it is a song by which the faithful praise the Lord and implore his mercy, it is ordinarily prayed by all, that is, alternately by the congregation and the choir or cantor.

As a rule each of the acclamations is said twice, but, because of the idiom of different languages, the music, or other circumstances, it may be said more than twice or a short verse (trope) may be interpolated. If the *Kyrie* is not sung, it is to be recited.

History. The presence of the Kyrie at Mass has a long and varied history. It originated in a litany of petition with the *Kyrie eleison* being the people's response after the deacon announced each intention. Transferred from after the homily to the beginning of the Roman Mass, the series of intentions announced by the deacon soon fell into disuse. Only the response remained. In time a trinitarian 3-3-3 structure developed.

An Acclamation. During Vatican II's revision of the Mass, there was much discussion regarding the retention of the Kyrie. Some desired its preservation for reasons of tradition and music. As a result, the Kyrie was incorporated into the penitential rite, depending on the particular option used. When the Confiteor is prayed, the Kyrie follows the penitential rite. In order not to duplicate the Confiteor (penitential) or the prayer of the faithful (litanic supplication), the function of the Kyrie is to be that of an acclamation praising God's goodness and mercy on behalf of all humankind. In accordance with the tradition of the church, the acclamation is addressed to Christ. Ordinarily each acclamation is made twice, although this number may be increased.

Expansions. On occasion, the acclamation may be expanded by means of a short verse which is called a trope. Such verses should be brief and addressed to Christ; it should not duplicate the penitential rite or the general intercessions.

Singing. Musical settings should be strong, energetic, and brief. A general rule might be not to sing the Kyrie if the Gloria is sung.

Glory to God

General Instruction of the Roman Missal

31. The *Gloria* is an ancient hymn in which the church, assembled in the Holy Spirit, praises and entreats the Father and the Lamb. It is sung by the congregation, or by the congregation alternately with the choir, or by the choir alone. If not sung, it is to be recited either by all together or in alternation.

The *Gloria* is sung or said on Sundays outside Advent and Lent, on solemnities and feasts, and in special, more solemn celebrations.

87. Either the priest or the cantors or even everyone together may begin the *Gloria*.

Origins and Liturgical Usage. The Gloria, originally composed in Greek, belongs to that body of early Christian hymns written by private individuals and modeled after the scriptural psalms. It is also known as the "Angelic Hymn" or the "Greater Doxology" as contrasted with the "Lesser Doxology" which concludes the eucharistic prayer. The text first appeared in the East, where it was sung during morning prayer. In the West it came to be used at Christmas and only by the bishop. In time the hymn was sung at all Sunday and martyr feastday liturgies at which the bishop presided. Only during the eleventh and twelfth centuries was its use extended to all Sunday and feastday liturgies.

Liturgical Tension. The presence of the Gloria among the introductory rites results in a certain degree of tension. Being a hymn, it should be sung. As Joseph Gelineau remarks: "To recite the Gloria in order to gain time is a kind of bastard solution from which the liturgical reform should have freed us" (*La Maison-Dieu* 100, 1969, p. 112). And yet to sing the Gloria is to lengthen further an already overly extended rite of preparation. Moreover, the frequent use of the Gloria tends to rob it of its festal character. This has led many authors to remark that it would advantageous if the Gloria were required only for very special feasts and occasions.

By Whom. The Gloria is sung by the entire assembly or by the assembly together with the choir. Since the Gloria is not an integral part of the liturgy, it may also be sung by the choir alone. This would be appropriate, for instance, on very solemn occasions. And yet such choir settings are to respect the inherent demand of the Gloria being part of the introductory rites of the Mass.

If recited, the Gloria is prayed by all together or in alternation. It is possible to alternate its recitation among various groups of the assembly or even between the presider and the others present.

A Good Beginning. The Gloria is begun by the presider (without any gesture as formerly required), by the cantor, the leader of song, the choir, or — it would seem — by some other minister. If the presider is not to intone the Gloria, he should be notified in advance to avoid duplication or confusion or both. This intonation, whether sung or recited, should be both joyful and firm so as to elicit immediate participation by the whole assembly.

Extra Dimensions. On more solemn occasions the hymn may be enhanced by the use of liturgical dance.

Celebrations with Children. Musical settings of this hymn may be used even if the texts differ from that found in the Sacramentary. For very small children the "Glory to the Father" is appropriate. Older children might be able to compose their own version of praise. Appropriate songs of praise to the Trinity might also be used. Refer to the *Directory for Masses with Children*, 31, 40.

Recommended Reading

Bishops' Committee on the Liturgy. *Music in Catholic Worship*, 66. Washington, D.C.: USCC, 1983.

————. "Notes on the Eucharistic Celebration: Gloria." *Newsletter* 7 (December 1971): 12.

Deiss, Lucien. *Spirit and Song of the New Liturgy*. Cincinnati: World Library of Sacred Music, 1976.

Emminghaus, Johannes H. *The Eucharist: Essence, Form, Celebration*. Collegeville, Minnesota: The Liturgical Press, 1978.

Federation of Diocesan Liturgical Commissions. *The Mystery of Faith*. Washington, D.C.: FDLC, 1981.

Gelineau, Joseph. *Learning to Celebrate*. Washington, D.C.: The Pastoral Press, 1985.

Opening Prayer

General Instruction of the Roman Missal

32. Next the priest invites the people to pray and together with him they observe a brief silence so that they may realize they are in God's presence and may call their petitions to mind. The priest then says the opening prayer, which custom has named the "collect." This expresses the theme of the celebration and the priest's words address a petition to God the Father through Christ in the Holy Spirit.

The people make the prayer their own and give their assent by the acclamation, *Amen.*

In the Mass only one opening prayer is said; this rule applies also to the prayer over the gifts and the prayer after communion.

The opening prayer ends with the longer conclusion, namely:

— if the prayer is directed to the Father:
We ask this (Grant this)
through our Lord Jesus Christ, your Son,
who lives and reigns with you and the Holy Spirit,
one God, for ever and ever;

— if it is directed to the Father, but the Son is
mentioned at the end:
Who lives and reigns with you and the Holy Spirit,
one God, for ever and ever;

— if directed to the Son:
You live and reign with the Father and the Holy Spirit,
one God, for ever and ever.

88. With his hands joined, the priest then invites the people to pray, saying: *Let us pray*. All pray silently with the priest for a while. Then the priest with hands outstretched says the opening prayer, at the end of which the people respond: *Amen*.

Structure and Names. One of the structural characteristics of the Roman Mass is the presence of three processions (entrance, presentation of the gifts, communion), each eventually concluded by a presidential prayer uttered in the name of all. These prayers are called "orations" from the Latin *oratio* meaning a discourse or speech.

The first oration has traditionally been given the name "collect." Opinions vary regarding the derivation of the term, but it may well be that it came from the fact that prayer was offered *super plebem collectam*, i.e., "over the people gathered together." It is now known as the opening prayer, a somewhat misleading designation. It is, however, the first oration of the celebration. Some refer to this oration as the prayer of the day.

Invitation to Prayer. Pausing momentarily after the Gloria, the priest extends the invitation, "Let us pray." The Sacramentary offers possible expansions for Sundays and major feasts. The presider, inviting the people, should not be looking into the book but rather at the assembly he is addressing. The presider's vocal quality should be warm, inviting, and sincere.

Silent Prayer. This period of silence is essential for the structural integrity of the prayer. Enough time must be allotted to allow the assembly to "realize they are in God's presence and...call their petitions to mind." It is only when adequate time is provided that any true meaning can be found in the words with which the priest often continues: "Hear the prayer of your family...." The presider's spoken prayer, following this quiet period, is to sum up the silent prayer of the assembly.

Spoken Prayer. After the silent prayer, the presider recapitulates aloud the prayers of the people. For Sundays and major feasts the Sacramentary provides both a translation of the original Latin texts as well as alternative prayers of English composition. Their structure comprises an address, most often to the Father, a petition usually of a very general nature, and then a concluding statement of praise known as a doxology.

During the prayer the priest "extends his hands" in such a way as to convey that it is God the Father to whom the prayer is ordinarily addressed. Thus a different type of gesture than that used for a greeting is in order.

Only this prayer, being the principal oration of the Mass, has a long conclusion which varies according to the prayer's structure. This conclusion should not be rushed. It is important. The priest does well to look at the people and to retard slightly the words "for ever and ever" so as to elicit a strong and resounding "Amen" from those present.

Although neither the English nor translated Latin formulas explicitly relate to the readings, liturgy planners and priests should make a judicious selection of the oration which best agrees with any particular motif of the celebration.

The introduction and the prayer may be sung, as is especially opportune on major feasts and celebrations. Some presiders who sing the opening prayer also sing the prayer over the gifts and the prayer after communion so as to preserve the symmetry of the liturgical structure. Although these prayers may be sung on a straight tone, their musical beauty is enhanced by using the oration tone provided in the musical section of the Sacramentary. For purposes of tone quality, it is traditional in English to *sing* "ah-men" even though we customarily *say* "a-men."

Masses with Children. The priest is not restricted to using the texts for the opening prayer, the prayer over the gifts, and the prayer after communion as found in the Sacramentary for a particular day. He may choose from the Sacramentary other presidential prayers as long as these accord with the liturgical season. He may even modify the official texts so that they may be more easily understood. However, the literary structure and function of the prayer is to be retained. Refer to the *Directory for Masses with Children*, 50, 51.

Late-Comers. The problem of seating late-comers is not easily resolved. Using ushers to find places for them during the introductory rites merely adds to the distraction. Some communities encourage late arrivals to remain standing at the rear of the building until the completion of the introductory rites. The people are then seated, and the Liturgy of the Word begins.

Recommended Reading

Deiss, Lucien. *Spirit and Song of the New Liturgy*. Cincinnati: World Library of Sacred Music, 1976.

Emminghaus, Johannes H. *The Eucharist: Essence, Form, Celebration*. Collegeville, Minnesota: The Liturgical Press, 1978.

Federation of Diocesan Liturgical Commissions. *The Mystery of Faith*. Washington, D.C.: FDLC, 1981.

Hughes, Kathleen. *The Opening Prayers of the Sacramentary: A Structural Study of the Prayers of Lent and Easter*. Ann Arbor, Michigan: University Microfilms, 1981.

2.

LITURGY OF
THE WORD

Overview

General Instruction of the Roman Missal

33. Readings from Scripture and the chants between the readings form the main part of the Liturgy of the Word. The homily, profession of faith, and general intercessions or prayer of the faithful expand and complete this part of the Mass. In the readings, explained by the homily, God is speaking to his people, opening up to them the mystery of redemption and salvation, and nourishing their spirit; Christ is present to the faithful through his own word. Through the chants the people make God's word their own and through the profession of faith affirm their adherence to it. Finally, having been fed by this word, they make their petitions in the general intercession for the needs of the Church and for the salvation of the whole world.

Origins. Although there is good reason to believe that the proclamation of God's Word accompanied the earliest Christian celebrations of the Eucharist, it was only after the separation of the Eucharist from the meal and probably through the influence of the Jewish synagogue service that a more structured format for this proclamation developed. As early as the second century, St. Justin wrote: "The memoirs of the apostles and the writings of the prophets are read for as long as time permits. When the reader has finished, the presider gives a discourse alerting the people and urging them to imitate these great teachings" (*First Apology*, 67).

Importance. The proclamation of the Word in the liturgical assembly is a central event in the life of the community since "in the liturgy God is speaking to his people and Christ is still proclaiming his Gospel" (*Constitution on the Liturgy*, 33). The Liturgy of the Word, therefore, is not a didactic exercise merely recalling past events. Rather, it is to be an experience of the living God's continuous revelation to us. It is to be a proclamation of the revelation of the Father. As such, the Liturgy of the Word stands intimately linked to the Liturgy of the Eucharist. Just as the celebration of God's Word is the oral proclamation of salvation, so the celebration of the Eucharist is the proclamation in action of the same mystery. Together they "form but one single act of worship" (*Constitution on the Sacred Liturgy*, 56). It is the same bread of life offered and shared in both.

Structure. The structure of the Liturgy of the Word is quite simple. Its dynamic is one of proclamation and response.

First Reading (Old Testament)	Proclamation
Responsorial Psalm	Response
Second Reading (New Testament)	Proclamation
Gospel Acclamation	Proclamation
Gospel	Proclamation
Homily	Proclamation
Profession of Faith	Response
General Intercessions	Response

Masses with Children. In accordance with the *Directory for Masses with Children* 17, some communities celebrate a special Liturgy of the Word with the children in an area apart from that used by the adults of the assembly. "Then, before the eucharistic liturgy begins, the children are led to the place where the adults have meanwhile celebrated their own Liturgy of the Word."

Recommended Reading

Bishops' Committee on the Liturgy. *Music in Catholic Worship*, 61. Washington, D.C.: USCC, 1983.

Collins, Patrick W. "Establishing the Importance of What Is Important: The Word." *Pastoral Music* 1, no. 4 (April-May 1977): 25-30. Reprinted in *Music in Catholic Worship: The NPM Commentary*. Ed. by Virgil C. Funk. Washington, D.C.: National Association of Pastoral Musicians, 1982.

Deiss, Lucien. *God's Word and God's People*. Trans. by Matthew J. O'Connell. Collegeville, Minnesota: The Liturgical Press, 1976.

Emminghaus, Johannes H. *The Eucharist: Essence, Form, Celebration*. Collegeville, Minnesota: The Liturgical Press, 1978.

Federation of Diocesan Liturgical Commissions. *The Mystery of Faith*. Washington, D.C.: FDLC, 1981.

Gelineau, Joseph. *Learning to Celebrate*. Washington, D.C.: The Pastoral Press, 1985.

Henchal, Michael. *Sunday Worship in Your Parish*. West Mystic, Connecticut: Twenty-Third Publications, 1980.

Huck, Gabe. *Preaching about the Mass*. Chicago: Liturgy Training Publications, 1992.

Huck, Gabe, ed., *Liturgy with Style and Grace*. Chicago: Liturgy Training Publications, 1984.

Jarrell, Stephen T. *Guide to the Sacramentary for Sundays and Festivals*. Chicago: Liturgy Training Publications, 1983.

Keifer, Ralph. *To Give Thanks and Praise*. Washington, D.C.: National Association of Pastoral Musicians, 1980.

The Lectionary

Call for Reform. The Second Vatican Council desired that "the treasures of the Bible...be opened up more lavishly, so that a richer share in God's Word may be provided for the faithful"; more specifically, "there is to be more reading from holy Scripture and it is to be more varied and apposite" (*Constitution on the Liturgy*, 51, 35.1).

Methods and Principles. In response to this request scholars spent five years studying ancient and contemporary systems for choosing liturgical readings. Their basic desire was to harmonize themes and yet present, with as much continuity as possible, the more significant sections of the Bible as requested by the Council.

The Revised Lectionary. The result of this labor was the publication in 1969 of the Lectionary for Mass. The book is divided into the following major sections: the temporal cycle; the sanctoral cycle; the commons; ritual Masses; Masses for various needs; votive Masses, and Masses for the dead. In 1981 there appeared a second edition of the book containing a number of additions and changes. In 1992 the National Conference of Catholic Bishops approved another revision.

Sunday Readings. These are extended over a three-year cycle (designated by the letters A, B, C) and form a unified whole. Each Sunday and major feast has three readings. The first is taken from the Old Testament except during the Easter season when, following ancient tradition, the selection is from the Acts of the Apostles. The second reading is taken from the epistles or the Book of Revelation. The essential feature differentiating each year is the Gospel. During Year A there is a semi-continuous reading from Matthew; Year B from Mark; Year C from Luke. Because of the brevity of Mark's Gospel, Year B is augmented by readings from John.

Weekday Readings. The ordinary weekdays have only two readings. The first reading is from the Old Testament, the epistles, or the Book of Revelation. The first readings after Epiphany and Pentecost are spread over a cycle of two years. The idea was to present extensive readings from the New Testament and limited readings from the First Testament so that the particular flavor of the various books would be appreciated by the faithful. The Gospel readings are taken from Mark for the first nine weeks, from Matthew for weeks ten to twenty-one, and from Luke for weeks twenty-two to thirty-four.

Translations. The American bishops previously authorized three versions of Scripture to be used in liturgical celebrations: the New American Bible; the Jerusalem Bible; and the Revised Standard Version (Catholic Edition). They have since authorized the New Revised Standard Version and the revised New Testament of the New American Bible. The Grail Psalter may also be employed for the psalmody.

Recommended Reading

Bishops' Committee on the Liturgy. *Proclaiming the Word: The Lectionary for Mass*. Liturgy Study Text Series 8. Washington, D.C.: USCC, 1982.

Emminghaus, Johannes H. *The Eucharist: Essence, Form, Celebration*. Collegeville, Minnesota: The Liturgical Press, 1978.

Keifer, Ralph. *To Hear and Proclaim: Introduction to the Lectionary with Commentary for Musicians and Priests*. Washington, D.C.: National Association of Pastoral Musicians, 1983.

Neve, Thomas. "The Shape of the New Lectionary." *The New Liturgy: A Comprehensive Introduction*. Ed. by Lancelot Sheppard. London: Longman & Todd, 1970.

Sloyan, Gerard S. "Overview of the *Lectionary for Mass: Introduction*." *The Liturgy Documents: A Parish Resource*. 3rd ed. Chicago: Liturgy Training Publications, 1991.

Choice of Readings

Sundays and Feasts. Although the Lectionary provides three readings for Sundays and a number of major feasts, individual conferences of bishops may decide, for pastoral reasons, to use only two of the three readings. Such, however, has not been approved in the United States. The pattern of three readings as found in the Lectionary is to be followed. Left to its own devices, a community can tend to choose the same books or passages of the Bible. Thus the full scope of biblical proclamation would be diminished.

Weekdays. Much more latitude is allowed for the choice of readings on weekdays. Although the church desires that the weekday course of readings be followed, pastoral needs allow for exceptions. Thus when the weekday cycle is interrupted by a greater feast or some other particular celebration, the priest may omit certain of the less significant weekday readings or combine them with other readings. In Masses for special groups the priest may choose from the readings of the week those most suitable for the group. He may also "choose readings not found in the current week, provided they are within the approved lectionary, are appropriate to the particular celebration, and are not chosen to the disadvantage of the ordinary weekday use of the weekday lectionary" (Bishops' Committee on the Liturgy, *Newsletter* 5 [December 1969]).

Non-Biblical Readings. It is the practice of some communities to substitute poems, prose selections, newspaper accounts, etc. for the scriptural readings. The *Third Instruction on the Constitution on the Sacred Liturgy* treats the legitimacy of this practice: "In no case is it allowed to substitute readings from other sacred or profane authors, ancient or modern. The homily has as its purpose to explain to the faithful the word of God just proclaimed..." (2a). It is the Word of God proclaimed through the Scriptures which calls us to conversion and salvation. In addition, the Scriptures possess an objectivity of faith common to the whole body of the church.

And yet non-biblical readings might be used to complement the inspired word of God, perhaps as an introduction to or as part of the homily. So used, these selections can serve to apply the eternal word of God to specific circumstances and times.

Masses with Children. The biblical readings are never to be omitted in Masses celebrated with children. Depending on the capabilities of the children present, it is permissible to reduce the number of readings. The Gospel, however, must always be proclaimed. If all the readings assigned to a particular day seem unsuited to the children, it is permissible to choose one or more readings from the Lectionary or from the Bible itself. However, the liturgical character of the day or season is to be taken into account. And in order to highlight the feast of a saint, an account of the saint's life may be read before the readings or incorporated into the homily. Refer to the *Directory for Masses with Children*, 41-43, 47.

In celebrations with children only approved translations of the Bible may be employed. Paraphrases of the sacred text are not permitted. The *Lectionary for Masses with Children,* approved by the National Conference of Catholic Bishops in 1991, fulfills this requirement.

Proclamation and Hearing the Word

Participation of the Assembly. According to the *Introduction to the Lectionary,* the members of the assembly "are to listen to the word of God with an inward and outward reverence that will bring them continuous growth in the spiritual life and draw them more deeply into the mystery they celebrate" (45). This presumes readers willing and able to communicate God's Word. It also presumes people willing and able to hear the message orally communicated through the reader. Faith, as we know, comes from hearing. People, therefore, should not be encouraged to follow the readings in participation aids or booklets which, in the words of the *Introduction*, are useful "for the faithful's preparation of the readings or for their personal meditation" (37). The proclamation of the Scriptures is a spoken event, not a communal reading exercise.

The people express their involvement in the proclamation through a concluding acclamation, i.e., "Thanks be to God," or, after the Gospel, "Praise to you, Lord Jesus Christ." This sign of assent is so important that at the conclusion of the readings the proclaimer (or even a person other than the reader for the non-Gospel selections) may sing "This is..." so that the assembly may give its acclamation in song as is fitting for all acclamations. Refer to the *Introduction to the Lectionary*, 18.

Silent Moments. Never to be rushed, the Liturgy of the Word calls for moments of silence during which prayerful reflection on the Word can take place. In such a way the scriptural message can take root and grow in the hearts of the people. Such times of silent activity can occur before the Liturgy of the Word begins, after the first two readings, and after the homily.

The Ambo. The ambo represents the dignity and uniqueness of God's Word as well as reflection upon that Word. Like its counterpart the altar, it is never used as a resting place for booklets, cards, hymnals, notes, and other such items. Furthermore, the ambo, by its nature, is reserved for the readings, the responsorial psalm, and the Easter *Exsultet*. It may also be used for the homily and for the giving of the individual intentions within the general intercessions.

In the early days of liturgical renewal it became customary in certain parishes to employ two lecterns: a major one for the proclamation of the Gospel and another, of lesser importance, for the proclamation of the other readings. And yet there is but one Word of God. Consequently there should only be one ambo from which all the readings are proclaimed.

The Lectionary. The Lectionary is the official liturgical book from which the readings are proclaimed. It is never to be replaced by sheets of paper, missalettes, or other aids which serve to help the people prepare for the liturgy.

Introducing the Readings. It is customary in many communities to preface the readings with an introduction. While such a practice is permissible, such comments should always "be simple, faithful to the text, brief, well prepared, and properly varied to suit the text they introduce" (*Introduction to the Lectionary*, 15). Such introductions should not paraphrase the readings but rather "set the stage" for the passage to follow by giving its background or by briefly relating it to the particular nature of the celebration or the assembly. Such introductions, however, are not always necessary.

What Not to Read. It is inappropriate for the reader to begin with a statement as "The first reading today is taken from the book of the prophet Ezekiel." People, we hope, know that this is the first reading. Sufficient is, "A reading from the book of the prophet Ezekiel." Furthermore, captions, i.e., the short sentences found in the Lectionary which are drawn from or summarize the readings, are provided as guides for selecting among the different readings when this is permitted. These captions, accordingly, are not to be read aloud.

Singing the Readings. While it is permissible to chant the readings, the music "must serve to stress the words, not obscure them" (*Introduction to the Lectionary*, 14). In deciding whether to chant a particular reading, the literary genre of the text must be considered to determine whether sung proclamation enhances and lends itself to the passage.

Communicating the Message. Some time ago the Bishops' Committee on the Liturgical Apostolate (the former name of the Bishops' Committee on the Liturgy) described the manner in which the Scriptures are to be proclaimed.

> All Scripture readings are to be proclamations, not mere recitations. Lectors and priest should approach the public reading of the Bible with full awareness that it is their honored task to render the official proclamation of the revealed word of God to His assembled holy people. The character of this reading is such that it must convey that special reverence which is due the Sacred Scriptures above all other words.
>
> 1. It is of fundamental importance that the reader communicate the fullest meaning of the passage. Without exaggerated emphasis or affectation, he must convey the particular significance of those words, phrases, clauses, or sentences which constitute the point being made. Careful phrasing and inflection are necessary to enable the listener to follow every thought and the relationship among them. Patterns of speech, especially monotonous patterns of speech, must be avoided, and the pattern of thought in the text must be adhered to. The message in all its meaning must be earnestly communicated.
>
> 2. The manner of speaking and tone of voice should be clear and firm, never indifferent or uncertain. The reader should not draw attention to himself either by being nervous and awkward or by being obviously conscious of a talent for dramatic reading. It is the message that should be remembered, not the one who reads it. The voice should be reverent without being unctuous, loud without shouting, authoritative without being offensive or overbearing. The pace must be geared to understanding — never hurried, never dragged.

3. By his voice, attitude, and physical bearing, the reader should convey the dignity and sacredness of the occasion. His role is that of a herald of the Word of God, his function to provide a meaningful encounter with the living Word. Perfection in this mission may not always be achieved, but it must always and seriously be sought (*Newsletter* 1, [December 1965]).

Concluding the Reading. At the conclusion of the text, the reader pauses for a moment, looks at the assembly, and says, "The Word of the Lord," from the Latin, *Verbum Domini*. On the First Sunday of Lent, 1993, this concluding statement was changed from the original translation, "This is the Word of the Lord."

It is the custom for many readers and proclaimers of the Gospel to hold the Lectionary up high while saying, "The Word (Gospel) of the Lord." Although the phrase refers to the text just proclaimed, it may also be argued that the book is the symbol of God's Word. If the book is held high, it should first be raised into position before the reader begins the phrase and should be lowered only after the acclamation. Whether the reader performs this gesture or not, he or she waits till the end of the acclamation before placing the book upon the ambo.

Suggested Resources for Planning the Liturgy of the Word

Freburger, William J. *This Is the Word of the Lord*. Notre Dame: Ave Maria Press, 1984. This contains eighty-five sets of readings arranged in dialogue form for three readers. Selections are given for Advent, Christmas, Lent, the Easter season, major feasts, and Ordinary Time.

A Workbook for Lectors and Gospel Readers. Chicago: Liturgy Training Publications. Published annually, this useful resource uses the New American Bible translation and provides helpful notes for those who will proclaim the texts.

First Reading

General Instruction of the Roman Missal

89. After the opening prayer, the reader goes to the
lectern for the first reading. All sit and make the
acclamation at the end.

Nature of the Reading. On all Sundays and solemnities of the
Lord, except during the Easter season, the first reading is taken
from the Old Testament, with the text having relationship to the
Gospel appointed for the day. Thus the reading may contain a
text quoted in the Gospel, be a prophecy fulfilled in the Gospel,
or stand in thematic continuity or contrast with the Gospel. On
weekdays, when there are only two readings, the first may be from
the Old Testament, but no attempt is made to relate the two
readings. The Old Testament proclamation recalls that Christians too share in the story of the Jewish people. Indeed a
fundamental unity exists between the two testaments since both
are the Word of God.

Some Suggestions. The skills of the reader not only require an
application of the principles of oral interpretation but also call
for an awareness of the demands of ritual action.

Since the Liturgy of the Word begins only after the opening
prayer, the reader should wait till the people have given their
Amen before moving to the place where the Lectionary is located.
With a deliberateness befitting the occasion the reader reverently
carries the book to the ambo.

Before beginning the reading, the reader must allow sufficient time for the assembly to sit. Waiting a few moments before
announcing the title of the reading not only gains the attention
of all but also allows the reader to focus his or her psychic energies
upon the task at hand.

Recommended Reading

Emminghaus, Johannes H. *The Eucharist: Essence, Form, Celebration*. Collegeville, Minnesota: The Liturgical Press, 1978.

Federation of Diocesan Liturgical Commissions. *The Mystery of Faith*. Washington, D.C.: FDLC, 1981.

Responsorial Psalm

General Instruction of the Roman Missal

36. After the first reading comes the responsorial psalm or gradual, an integral part of the Liturgy of the Word. The psalm as a rule is drawn from the Lectionary because the individual psalm texts are directly connected with the individual readings: the choice of psalm depends therefore on the readings. Nevertheless, in order that the people may be able to join in the responsorial psalm more readily, some texts of responses and psalms have been chosen, according to the different seasons of the year and classes of saints, for optional use, whenever the psalm is sung, in place of the text corresponding to the reading.

The psalmist or cantor of the psalm sings the verses of the psalm at the lectern or other suitable place. The people remain seated and listen, but also as a rule take part by singing the response, except when the psalm is sung straight through without the response.

The psalm when sung may be either the psalm assigned in the Lectionary or the gradual from the *Graduale Romanum* or the responsorial psalm or the psalm with *Alleluia* as the response from *The Simple Gradual* in the form they have in those books.

Introduction to the Lectionary for Mass

19. The responsorial psalm, also called the gradual, has great liturgical and pastoral significance because it is an "integral part of the Liturgy of the Word." Accordingly the people must be continually instructed on the way to perceive the word of God speaking in the psalms and to turn these psalms into

the prayer of the Church. This, of course, "will be achieved more readily if a deeper understanding of the psalms, in the meaning in which they are used in the liturgy, is more diligently promoted among he clergy and communicated to all the faithful by means of appropriate catechesis."

20. As a rule the responsorial psalm should be sung. There are two established ways of singing the psalm after the first reading: responsorially and directly. In responsorial singing, which, as far as possible, is to be given preference, the psalmist or cantor of the psalm sings the psalm verse and the whole congregation joins in by singing the response. In direct singing of the psalm there is no intervening response by the community; either the psalmist or cantor of the psalm sings the psalm alone as the community listens or else all sing it together.

21. The singing of the psalm, or even of the response alone, is a great help toward understanding and meditating on the psalm's spiritual meaning.

To foster the congregation's singing, every means available in the various cultures is to be employed. In particular use is to be made of all the relevant options provided in the Order of Readings for Mass regarding responses corresponding to the different liturgical seasons.

22. When not sung, the psalm after the reading is to be recited in a manner conducive to meditation on the word of God.

The responsorial psalm is sung or recited by the psalmist or cantor at the lectern.

History and Name. Following the practice of the Jewish synagogue, the community traditionally replies to a scriptural reading by singing a psalm or biblical canticle. In Rome, a subdeacon or cantor mounted the ambo and chanted the text, which came to be called the gradual, a name taken from the steps, i.e., *gradus*, of the ambo. Today it is called the responsorial psalm, a designation expressing the structural nature of the text.

Function. Although some call attention to the meditative quality of the psalm, reflection is not its primary function. Rather, the psalm serves as the people's response to the reading just proclaimed. The scriptural message is to reverberate in the assembly whose members together acknowledge and respond to the Word of God by using the Word of God.

Principles for Selection. The selection of the responsorial psalms found in the Lectionary was done with the utmost care. Certain general principles were followed. Thus, a psalm is used for a response if the Scriptures for the day quote the psalm, if a literary reference is made to the psalm in the first reading, or if the psalm more clearly illustrates what is proclaimed in the reading. Additionally, psalms having a connection with a particular liturgical season are used during that season, e.g., the penitential psalms during Lent. Furthermore, a selection of psalms appropriate to each season of the year is also given.

Sing the Psalm. The *Order of Mass* considers it normative that the responsorial psalm be sung. The reason is threefold:

1. the genre of the psalms as lyrical compositions calls for singing;

2. the psalm is a response to the spoken word, and ritual structure does not customarily respond to speech with more speech;

3. this is the only time in the liturgy when a psalm is used for its own sake and not to accompany a ritual action.

Every effort, therefore, is to be made to sing the psalm response. To sing a hymn at the presentation of the gifts and not to sing the responsorial psalm does violence to the musical structure of the celebration.

41

Choosing the Text. In selecting texts, music planners may use:

1. the psalm as appointed for the day in the Lectionary;

2. one of the common psalms found in the Lectionary for the various liturgical seasons: this eliminates the practical problem of having the people, cantor, or choir learn a new musical setting for each celebration;

3. the gradual as found in the *Graduale Romanum* or the responsorial psalm in the *Graduale Simplex* (both books, however, contain Latin texts set to plainsong melodies);

4. other "psalms and antiphons in English, as supplements to the *Simple Gradual*, including psalms arranged in responsorial form, metrical and similar versions of the psalms, provided they are used in accordance with the principles of the *Simple Gradual* and are selected in harmony with the liturgical season, feast, or occasion" (*Appendix to the* General Instruction *for the Dioceses of the United States of America*, 36.).

Options for Singing the Psalms. The psalmody may be rendered in a variety of ways:

1. the cantor or choir sings the verses and, after each verse or set of verses, all respond with the antiphon;

2. the psalm verses are alternated by two sections of the assembly;

3. the psalm verses are sung straight through by the assembly;

4. the psalm verses are sung straight through by
the cantor or choir.

Other Alternatives. Numerous hymn texts are close paraphrases of the psalms. If the choice is between not singing the psalm or using a hymn paraphrase, many prefer the latter option. In no case, however, should a text not drawn from the psalter be used since the liturgical structure is to respond to God's Word with God's Word.

In the absence of a cantor or choir it is possible, though not ideal, to read the verses with a soft instrumental background. The verses are, perhaps, best rendered by a person other than the reader. In this way the character of the psalm as a response rather than a prolongation of the reading will be apparent. The verses should be read slowly, clearly, and in such a way as to invite the assembly's response which, if at all possible, is sung.

Masses with Children. "Verses of psalms, carefully selected in accord with the understanding of children, or singing in the form of psalmody...should be sung between the readings. The children should always have a part in this singing, but sometimes a reflective silence may be substituted for the singing. If only a single reading is chosen, the singing may follow the homily" (*Directory for Masses with Children*, 46).

Recommended Reading

Bishops' Committee on the Liturgy. *Music in Catholic Worship*, 63. Washington, D.C.: USCC, 1983.

————. "Notes on the Eucharistic Celebration." *Newsletter* 9 (April 1973).

Bugnini, G. "The Responsorial Psalm: Recited or Sung?" In Bishops' Committee on the Liturgy, *Newsletter* 12 (April 1976).

Deiss, Lucien. *Spirit and Song of the New Liturgy*. Cincinnati: World Library of Sacred Music, 1976.

————. "The Gradual Psalm." In *The New Liturgy: A Comprehensive Introduction*. Ed. by Lancelot Sheppard. London: Longman & Todd, 1970.

Emminghaus, Johannes H. *The Eucharist: Essence, Form, Celebration*. Collegeville, Minnesota: The Liturgical Press, 1978.

Federation of Diocesan Liturgical Commissions. *The Mystery of Faith*. Washington, D.C.: FDLC, 1981.

Gelineau, Joseph. *Learning to Celebrate*. Washington, D.C.: The Pastoral Press, 1985.

National Conference of Catholic Bishops. "Appendix to the *General Instruction* for the Dioceses of the United States of America," 36. Washington, D.C.: USCC, 1982.

Shepherd, Massey. "Responsorial Psalmody. The Gradual." *The Psalms in Christian Worship: A Practical Guide*. Collegeville, Minnesota: The Liturgical Press, 1976.

Second Reading

General Instruction of the Roman Missal

91. Then if there is a second reading before the gospel, the reader reads it at the lectern as before. All sit and listen and make the acclamation at the end.

Selection of Texts. On Sundays and certain major feasts another reading, usually quite brief, occurs before the proclamation of the Gospel. It is taken from the New Testament letters, the Acts of the Apostles, or the Book of Revelation. Most frequently this passage has no specific relationship to the other two readings. It is a semi-continuous reading ordinarily occurring on the Sundays of the year. However, during some of the more important liturgical seasons, the selections correspond to the mystery being celebrated, as, for example, during the Easter season when we read from the First Letter of Peter, which explains the implications of baptism into Christ.

Number of Readers. Whenever possible, the readings should be proclaimed by two different readers. Such a practice not only allows more people to share in this ministry but also adds variety to the proclamation.

Recommended Reading

Federation of Diocesan Liturgical Commissions. *The Mystery of Faith*. Washington, D.C.: FDLC, 1981.

Gospel Acclamation

General Instruction of the Roman Missal

37. As the season requires, the *Alleluia* or another chant follows the second reading.

a. The *Alleluia* is sung in every season outside Lent. It is begun either by all present or by the choir or cantor; it may then be repeated. The verses are taken from the Lectionary or the *Graduale*.

b. The other chant consists of the verse before the gospel or another psalm or tract, as found in the Lectionary or the *Graduale*.

38. When there is only one reading before the gospel:

a. during a season calling for the *Alleluia*, there is an option to use either the psalm with *Alleluia* as the response, or the responsorial psalm and the *Alleluia* with its verse, or just the psalm or just the *Alleluia*.

b. during the season when the *Alleluia* is not allowed, either the responsorial psalm or the verse before the gospel may be used.

39. If not sung, the *Alleluia* or the verse before the gospel may be omitted.

Introduction to the Lectionary for Mass

23. The *Alleluia* or, as the liturgical season requires, the verse before the gospel, is also a "rite or act standing by itself." It serves as the assembled faithful's greeting of welcome to the Lord who is about to speak to them and as an expression of their faith through song.

The *Alleluia* or the verse before the gospel must be sung and during it all stand. It is not to be sung only

45

by the cantor who intones it or by the choir, but by
the whole congregation together.

An Ancient Tradition. The word "Alleluia," from the Hebrew "Praise Yahweh," is often found in the Bible, especially in certain of the psalms. The expression was incorporated into the Christian liturgy at an early date where, at least in the West, it became a sign of joy, especially the joy of Easter. In the Liturgy of the Word, the people sing the Alleluia to praise the risen Lord, who will speak in the Gospel.

A Sung Acclamation. Unlike the psalm after the first reading, the Alleluia is not a response. Rather, it is an acclamation, a joyful shout of readiness and anticipation. As such it looks forward to what is to come.

Since recited liturgical acclamations are rarely acclamatory, the Alleluia is to be sung. It is hard to imagine when this would not be possible. Nevertheless, if not sung, it is replaced by a few moments of silence.

Method of Singing. The cantor, or perhaps the choir, sings the Alleluia two or three times. The acclamation is then repeated by all. The verse, relating to Christ, the day, or even of a general nature, is then sung or, less ideally, recited. All repeat the Alleluia. Simply to omit the verse often weakens the impact of this musical moment. Some communities at times substitute a hymn text addressed to Christ and incorporating the Alleluia. If such is done, the content and acclamatory nature of this structural element is to be respected.

Standing. In accord with ancient tradition, all stand for the Gospel as well as its preparatory acclamation. This is a sign of readiness, of baptismal dignity, of resurrection with Christ. The simple rising of the ministers suffices as a signal for others to do so. Ordinarily, the singing of the Alleluia should not begin until all are standing and prepared for the acclamation.

During Lent. The Alleluia, because of its paschal connotations, is not sung during Lent, when it is replaced by an equivalent formula.

The Sequence. In the early church, the singing of the Alleluia concluded with a long vocal passage known as the *jubilus*. To help the soloist remember the melody, words were added to the notes. Eventually this practice gave rise to a body of prose and then poetic texts sung as units independent of the Alleluia. These "sequences" especially flourished in northern Europe.

Today the sequence is required only on Easter and Pentecost. Two versions, prose and poetry, are given in the Lectionary. Of very minor liturgical importance, they are best recited, perhaps with a discreet instrumental background. The recitation should be by a person other than the reader since the sequence is not a proclamation of God's Word.

Recommended Reading

Bishops' Committee on the Liturgy. *Music in Catholic Worship*, 55. Washington, D.C.: USCC, 1983.

———. "Notes on Eucharistic Celebration." *Newsletter* 9 (April 1973).

———. "The Gospel Acclamation." *Newsletter* 21 (October 1985): 39.

Deiss, Lucien. *Spirit and Song of the New Liturgy*. Cincinnati: World Library of Sacred Music, 1976.

———. "The Alleluia, or the Processional for the Gospel." In *The New Liturgy: A Comprehensive Introduction.* Ed. by Lancelot Sheppard. London: Longman & Todd, 1970.

Emminghaus, Johannes H. *The Eucharist: Essence, Form, Celebration*. Collegeville, Minnesota: The Liturgical Press, 1978.

Federation of Diocesan Liturgical Commissions. *The Mystery of Faith*. Washington, D.C.: FDLC, 1981.

The Gospel

General Instruction of the Roman Missal

93. During the singing of the *Alleluia* or other chant, if incense is being used, the priest puts some into the censer. Then with hands joined he bows before the altar and says softly the prayer, *Almighty God, cleanse my heart.*

94. If the Book of the Gospels is on the altar, he takes it and goes to the lectern, the servers, who may carry the censer and candles, walking ahead of him.

95. At the lectern the priest opens the book and says: *The Lord be with you*. Then he says: *A reading from...*, making the sign of the cross with his thumb on the book and on his forehead, mouth and breast. If incense is used, he then incenses the book. After the acclamation of the people, he proclaims the gospel and at the end kisses the book, saying softly: *May the words of the gospel wipe away our sins*. After the reading the people make the acclamation customary to the region.

Introduction to the Lectionary for Mass

17. Of all the rites connected with the liturgy of the word, the reverence due to the gospel reading must receive special attention. Where there is a Book of the Gospels that has been carried in by the deacon or reader during the entrance procession, it is most fitting that the deacon or a priest, when there is no deacon, take the book from the altar and carry it to the lectern. He is preceded by servers with candles and incense or other symbols of reverence that may be customary. As the faithful stand and acclaim the Lord, they show honor to the Book of the Gospels. The deacon who is to read the gospel, bowing in front of the one presiding, asks and receives the blessing. When no deacon is present, the priest, bowing before the altar, prays quietly: *Almighty God, cleanse my heart...*

At the lectern the one who proclaims the gospel greets the people, who are standing, and announces the reading as he makes the sign of the cross on forehead, mouth and breast. If incense is used, he next incenses the book, then reads the gospel. When finished, he kisses the book, saying the appointed words quietly.

> Even if the gospel itself is not sung, it is
> appropriate for *The Lord be with you, A reading from
> the holy gospel...*, and at the end *This is the Gospel of
> the Lord* to be sung, in order that the assembly may
> also sing its acclamations. This is a way both of
> bringing out the importance of the gospel reading
> and of stirring up the faith of those who hear it.

Christ Speaks. Although God speaks to us in the totality of the Scriptures, it is especially in the proclamation of the Gospel that the Lord Jesus is present in his Word. For this reason the Gospel is the only reading traditionally accompanied by a procession and other special signs of honor.

The Proclaimer of the Gospel. Whereas the other readings may be proclaimed by any qualified person, the Gospel is reserved to ordained ministers. The liturgical proclamation of all the readings is a ministerial rather than a presidential task. Thus a deacon or, in his absence, a priest other than the presider proclaims the Gospel. Only in their absence is this done by the presiding priest.

Before the Procession. If no Book of the Gospels is used, it is necessary for the reader to return the Lectionary to the altar from where it will be taken for the Gospel procession. When, however, there is a Gospel Book, then the Lectionary should be removed from the ambo and placed in a fitting location.

If incense is to be used, it is placed in the censer and is silently blessed with the sign of the cross.

The first private devotional prayer of the Mass follows. If a person other than the presider is to proclaim the Gospel, he approaches the presider, bows low, and requests a blessing, which is given in a low voice by the presider. If the presiding priest is to give the Gospel reading, he approaches the altar, bows low, and says the "Almighty God," a shortened version of a prayer of medieval origin. According to the translation of the *General Instruction* appearing in the most recent editions of the Sacramentary, the prayer of the priest is said "inaudibly." It is only after the blessing or the prayer that the book is taken from the altar.

The Procession. The number of participants, signs of honor, and the route should vary in accord with the solemnity of the occasion. Details should be planned and even practiced in advance. The ministers arrive at the ambo as the Alleluia is being concluded.

Introducing and Concluding the Text. The minister without extending his hands addresses the assembly with the usual greeting. After the response, he announces the Gospel and, during the people's acclamation, makes the triple sign of the cross, which expresses that:

1. our minds are to be receptive to Christ's Word,

2. our lips are to profess the Word, and

3. our hearts are to love the Word.

Although not required by the rubrics, it is customary for all to make this sign. If incense is used, the book is now incensed with three swings of the censer.

At the conclusion of the Gospel, the minister pauses for a moment and then proclaims, "The Gospel of the Lord." (As with the first and second readings, this concluding statement was changed from the original translation, "This is the Gospel of the Lord," on the First Sunday of Lent, 1993). All give the response, "Praise to you, Lord Jesus Christ." Then he kisses the book and quietly says, "May the words of the Gospel wipe away our sins," a text dating from the Middle Ages. The book may then be presented to another minister who returns it to a fitting place of honor. Or, more preferably, with pages open it is placed upon the ambo since the homilist will be preaching on the Word of God which has just been proclaimed. In no case is the book summarily relegated to a bottom shelf of the ambo.

Recommended Reading

Emminghaus, Johannes H. *The Eucharist: Essence, Form, Celebration*. Collegeville, Minnesota: The Liturgical Press, 1978.

Homily

Introduction to the Lectionary for Mass

24. Through the course of the liturgical year the
homily sets forth the mysteries of faith and the
standards of the Christian life on the basis of the
sacred text. Beginning with the Constitution on the
Liturgy, the homily as part of the liturgy of the word
has been repeatedly and strongly recommended and
in some cases it is obligatory. As a rule it is to be
given by the one presiding. The purpose of the
homily at Mass is that the spoken word of God and
the liturgy of the eucharist may together become "a
proclamation of God's wonderful works in the history
of salvation, the mystery of Christ." Through the
readings and homily Christ's paschal mystery is
proclaimed; through the sacrifice of the Mass it
becomes present. Moreover Christ himself is also
always present and active in the preaching of his
Church.

Whether the homily explains the biblical word of
God proclaimed in the readings or some other text of
the liturgy, it must always lead the community of the
faithful to celebrate the Eucharist wholeheartedly "so
that they may hold fast in their lives to what they
have grasped by their faith." From this living
explanation, the word of God proclaimed in the
readings and the Church's celebration of the day's
liturgy will have greater impact. But this demands
that the homily be truly the fruit of meditation,
carefully prepared, neither too long nor too short,
and suited to all those present, even children and the
uneducated.

At a concelebration, the celebrant or one of the
concelebrants as a rule gives the homily.

25. On the prescribed days, that is, Sundays and
holydays of obligation, there must be a homily in all
Masses celebrated with a congregation, even Masses
on the preceding evening. There is also to be a

homily in Masses with children and with special groups.

A homily is strongly recommended on the weekdays of Advent, Lent, and the Easter season for the sake of the faithful who regularly take part in the celebration of Mass; also on other feasts and occasions when a large congregation is present.

26. The priest celebrant gives the homily either at the chair, standing or sitting, or at the lectern.

27. Any necessary announcements are to be kept completely separate from the homily; they must take place following the prayer after communion.

Unaffected Speech. The word "homily" derives from the Greek *homilia,* meaning "a familiar talk," i.e., a type of speech different from a solemn oratorical discourse.

Continuation of God's Word. Starting from the biblical text, the homily applies God's Word to the concrete needs and circumstances to Christian life today. As such, it is fundamentally neither exegesis, moralization, nor didacticism. Rather, it is the proclamation of God's saving deeds in Christ to a people both converted and converting. It is the unfolding of the mystery of Christ proclaimed in the Scriptures and manifested among us today. The homily is an integral part of the celebration and finds its natural conclusion in the Liturgy of the Eucharist.

By Whom. Ordinarily the homily is given by the presiding priest or, continuing a long-standing tradition of the church, by the deacon. The *Third Instruction on the Constitution on the Liturgy* recalls that "the congregation is to refrain from comments, attempts at dialogue, or anything similar" (2). And yet, according to the Code of Canon Law, canon 766, lay persons may preach "in a church or oratory if it is necessary in certain circumstances or if it is useful in particular cases according to the prescriptions of the conference of bishops and with due regard" for the reservation of the homily to a priest or deacon.

Preaching from the Text. The foundation and starting point of the homily is, of course, the scriptural text. Yet the homilist need not, for example on Sundays, attempt to touch upon much less synthesize all the readings. In homily preparation the overall series of readings appointed for a season is to be considered. Furthermore, the responsorial psalm or another biblical text found in the day's liturgy may, on occasion, be the basis for the preaching. (See *General Instruction*, 41.)

Input and Evaluation. Liturgy planning sessions offer an opportunity for providing input to the homilist. Some communities have initiated various forms of feedback groups to help the homilist define his skills and enhance his effectiveness.

Sign of the Cross. Since the homily is not an appendage to but an integral part of the liturgy, the practice of beginning and ending the homily with the sign of the cross is not recommended. This not only appears to destroy the essential link between the readings and the homily but also duplicates the sign of the cross made toward the beginning of the introductory rites.

Masses with Children. If the presiding priest is unable to adapt his homily to the mentality of children, he may, with the consent of the pastor, allow another adult to speak after the Gospel. Dialogue homilies are also permitted. Refer to the *Directory for Masses with Children*, 24, 48.

Recommended Reading

Emminghaus, Johannes H. *The Eucharist: Essence, Form, Celebration*. Collegeville, Minnesota: The Liturgical Press, 1978.

Federation of Diocesan Liturgical Commissions. *The Mystery of Faith*. Washington, D.C.: FDLC, 1981.

Huck, Gabe. *Preaching about the Mass*. Chicago: Liturgy Training Publications, 1992.

LaVerdiere, Eugene. "The Art of Proclamation." *Church* 8, no. 2 (Summer 1992).

National Conference of Catholic Bishops. *Fulfilled in Your Hearing: The Homily in the Sunday Assembly*. Washington, D.C.: USCC, 1982.

Searle, Mark. "Below the Pulpit: The Lay Contribution to the Homily." *Assembly* 7, no. 2 (November 1980): 110.

Skudlarek, William. "No Preaching, Please!" *Modern Liturgy* 12, no. 7 (October 1985): 12-14.

Profession of Faith

General Instruction of the Roman Missal

43. The symbol or profession of faith in the celebration of Mass serves as a way for the people to respond and to give their assent to the word of God heard in the readings and through the homily and for them to call to mind the truths of faith before they begin to celebrate the Eucharist.

44. Recitation of the profession of faith by the priest together with the people is obligatory on Sundays and solemnities. It may be said also at special, more solemn occasions.

If it is sung, as a rule all are to sing it together or in alternation.

98. The profession of faith is said by the priest together with the people (see no. 44). At the words, *by the power of the Holy Spirit*, etc. all bow; on the solemnities of the Annunciation and Christmas all kneel.

Beginnings. The profession of faith had its origins in the celebration of baptism with a series of three questions and answers dealing respectively with the three persons of the Trinity. A threefold immersion or dipping into the water accompanied this series. In the course of time more complex and theologically developed expansions of the text arose in both East and West.

The Nicene Creed. The creed presently professed at Mass was formulated at the Council of Chalcedon (451), and eventually came to be called the Niceno-Constantinopolitan Creed since it expresses the articles of faith professed at the Councils of Nicea

(325) and Constantinople (381). More simply known as the Nicene Creed, it is also called the "symbol of faith," i.e., a compilation of beliefs by which Christians are identified.

Into the Liturgy. As a reaction to various Christological heresies, the Nicene Creed entered the eastern liturgies as early as the fifth century. Traveling to the West by way of Spain, the liturgical use of the formula spread throughout the Carolingian Empire under the influence of Charlemagne. When Emperor Henry II reached Rome in 1014 for his coronation, he expressed surprise that the Creed was missing from the Mass as celebrated in that city. Although he was informed that Rome was never troubled with doctrinal error and therefore had no need for a frequent recitation of the text, Pope Benedict VIII incorporated it into the Roman Mass.

A Response in Faith to the Word. As an expression of belief, the creed is professed by the whole assembly in response to the word just proclaimed in the readings and preached in the homily. Although the whole celebration of Word and Eucharist is an affirmation of faith, the presence of the creed articulates this faith in explicit terms. It is a moment to give a resounding "yes" to the unending and marvelous works of God on our behalf.

The Apostles' Creed. Some have argued for the use of other professions of faith, especially the more simple Apostles' Creed, as was, for example, the desire of many at the 1967 Synod of Bishops. And yet the Nicene Creed's strong profession of faith in the divinity of Christ resulted in its exclusive retention by the *Order of Mass*. Nonetheless, several countries have received permission to use the Apostles' Creed as an option. The bishops of the United States, however, in 1978 voted not to request this permission from Rome.

Masses with Children. The *Directory for Masses with Children* (31, 49) allows the Apostles' Creed to be used because it is part of the children's catechetical formation; it also gives approval for song paraphrases.

A Corporate Expression of Faith. The English version of the creed translates the Latin singular "I believe," i.e., *Credo*, into the plural "We believe" and thus agrees with the introduction found in many of the eastern liturgies. As used at Mass, the creed professes the faith shared by a community of believers.

Recited or Sung. The creedal text, not possessing a lyrical quality easily lending itself to musical settings, is best recited, as has long been the general rule in the East. The whole assembly together says the formula.

Nevertheless, when sung to a simple melody, a certain degree of forceful unity is possible. In this case the text is sung by all together or in alternation. It would appear that the rubrics allow the creed to be rendered by the choir alone on certain extraordinary occasions. Concert versions, however, are always unacceptable.

Beginning the Text. The intonation, which need not be given by the presider, should not begin till all are standing and ready after the homily. If the priest or another minister intones with the use of a microphone, this person's voice should be lowered once the assembly begins. The intonation should be strong and steady. It should set the pace for what is to follow.

Bodily Involvement. Although often overlooked in practice, the custom of the whole assembly bowing at the words "by the power of the Holy Spirit..." is mentioned by the *General Instruction* (98). When reverently done, the gesture contributes to the bodily involvement of all participants in the choreography of the celebration. The same is true for kneeling during these words on the feasts of Christmas and the Annunciation.

Recommended Reading

Bishops' Committee on the Liturgy. *Music in Catholic Worship*, 69. Washington, D.C.: 1983.

Crichton, J. D. *Christian Celebration: The Mass*. London: Geoffrey Chapman, 1971.

Deiss, Lucien. *Spirit and Song of the New Liturgy*. Cincinnati: World Library of Sacred Music, 1976.

Emminghaus, Johannes H. *The Eucharist: Essence, Form, Celebration*. Collegeville, Minnesota: The Liturgical Press, 1978.

Federation of Diocesan Liturgical Commissions. *The Mystery of Faith*. Washington, D.C.: FDLC, 1981.

Gelineau, Joseph. *Learning to Celebrate*. Washington, D.C.: The Pastoral Press, 1985.

Huck, Gabe, ed. *Liturgy with Style and Grace*. Chicago: Liturgy Training Publications, 1984.

General Intercessions

Introduction to the Lectionary for Mass

30. Enlightened by God's word and in a sense responding to it, the assembly of the faithful prays in the general intercessions as a rule for the need of the universal Church and the local community, for the salvation of the world and those oppressed by any burden, and for special categories of people.

The celebrant introduces the prayer; the deacon, another minister, or some of the faithful may propose intentions that are short and phrased with a measure of flexibility. In these petitions, "the people, exercising their priestly function, make intercession for all," with the result that, as the Liturgy of the Word has its full effects in them, they are better prepared to proceed to the Liturgy of the Eucharist.

31. For the general intercessions the celebrant presides at the chair and the intentions are announced at the lectern.

The congregation takes part in the general intercessions while standing and by saying or singing a common response after each intention or by silent prayer.

A Restoration. Just as the Jewish synagogue service included a series of petitionary prayers for the community, so at an early

57

period a series of prayers for various intentions came to conclude the Liturgy of the Word. Due to a number of complex and unfortunate liturgical changes, these prayers disappeared from the Roman Mass until restored by the post-Vatican II revision of the liturgy.

A Variety of Names. The prayer is known by several names. It is called the "Prayer of the Faithful" since in the early church the catechumens, not allowed to participate in the remainder of the liturgy, were formally dismissed before this prayer. It is more properly called the "General Intercessions" or "Universal Prayer" since the prayer entreats God on behalf of people and their needs everywhere. In England it is termed the "Bidding Prayers," a phrase deriving from a series of petitionary prayers at times joined to the sermon in the Church of England.

Function and Structure. The general intercessions form a logical conclusion to what has just been celebrated. Having heard and been nourished by the Word of God, the assembly responds by remembering and praying for the church and the world. The structure is threefold: an initial invitation to pray, the petitions and their response, and a closing prayer.

The Invitation to Pray. The priest, standing at the presider's chair, addresses the people and invites them to pray. There is no initial greeting.

This invitation should be short and is not to become a prayer in itself. Its content should link the petitions to follow with the scripture readings or the feast being celebrated. If this has already been done at the conclusion of the homily and when the intercessions follow immediately, a simple "Let us pray" suffices.

The Petitions and the Response. Ordinarily the intentions are:

1. for the church;

2. for the world and the nation;

3. for those oppressed by any kind of need;

4. for the local community.

Yet there is no need to be overly rigid in following this pattern when circumstances and occasions suggest otherwise. At least one petition, however, should be selected from each category since a balance between universality and particularity must be maintained. Ordinarily five or six petitions are sufficient.

The intentions are to announce petitions and are not to be statements of praise, adoration, or thanksgiving. Nor should they be directed to God. In formulating the intentions care should be taken that they not be didactic or divisive in character. They should be brief, concrete, and specific, with one idea in each intention.

In formulating the intentions, liturgy planners need consider their literary structure. The following phraseologies are commonly used.

1. For the sick who imitate Christ .... let us pray.

2. That the sick may be healed by .... let us pray.

3. For the sick that their sufferings ...... let us pray.

4. For the sick that they may be .... let us pray.

The last form, however, is somewhat cumbersome. But whichever format is employed, its use should be consistent throughout in order to obtain symmetry and rhythmic flow.

The intentions are normally led by a minister other than the presider. They are preferably given by the deacon at the ambo or standing next to the presider. If another minister announces the intentions, this is done at a convenient place, ordinarily the ambo.

Since it is often very difficult to invite spontaneous petitions in larger assemblies, some parishes have petition boxes where their members deposit written intentions. These are then formulated and summarized for public use at the next week's liturgy.

It is important that an adequate period of silent prayer occur at the end of the petitions. Such may be indicated by the person announcing the petitions or, preferably, simply left to the understanding of the people.

The people respond to each intention with a short formula whose wording should obviously not change throughout the intercessions. This response may take the form of supplication, e.g., "Hear us, O Lord," or of acclamation, e.g., "Glory to God on high." If only a few different responsorial forms are used throughout a particular season of the year, participation is more easily elicited. A few seconds of silence may prove advantageous before the leader gives the cue for the response. This allows the assembly to pray silently for the intention announced.

The Concluding Prayer. The priest concludes the litany by requesting God to look favorably upon the prayer of all assembled. As such this oration summarizes what has preceded. The prayer is addressed to God the Father in accord with traditional Roman usage. It concludes with, "...through Christ our Lord." To distinguish this prayer from the major presidential prayers no uplifting of the hands is directed by the rubrics; nor is it prefixed by the invitation "Let us pray" since this is what the people have been doing all along.

Many presiders improvise this prayer. Nonetheless, true improvisation is a gift not bestowed upon all. Where previous preparation has been lacking, vapid meanderings are often inflicted upon the people.

Music. The general intercessions are litanic in form, and litanies are more effective when sung. Their impact is greater. Thus the intentions, if formulated with simplicity and balance, are enhanced by singing. But it is especially the response which can be invigorated by song. Should the petitions be spoken, the problem of providing a musical cue can be solved if the cantor sings "We pray to the Lord" before each sung response, which the choir might further enhance by providing harmony.

Creativity. Although numerous publications offer examples of the general intercessions, these should be considered as models for the local community's creative efforts. The intentions should reflect current events in the life of the world, the church, the nation, and the local community. After the texts have been formulated, they should be placed in an attractive binder for use by the ministers. Slides, dance, and other visual aids can contribute to the impact of the intentions.

Recommended Reading

Bishops' Committee on the Liturgy. *General Intercessions.* Washington, D.C.: USCC, 1971.

———. "General Intercessions." *Newsletter* 11 (March 1975).

———. "Structure of the General Intercessions." *Newsletter* 6 (September-October 1970).

Ciferni, Andrew D. "General Intercessions in the Celebration of the Eucharist: A Writer's Guide." *Federation of Diocesan Liturgical Commissions Newsletter* 18, no. 6 (November-December 1991): 52-54.

Crichton, J. D. *Christian Celebration: The Mass.* London: Geoffrey Chapman, 1971.

Deiss, Lucien. *Spirit and Song of the New Liturgy.* Cincinnati: World Library of Sacred Music, 1976.

Emminghaus, Johannes H. *The Eucharist: Essence, Form, Celebration.* Collegeville, Minnesota: The Liturgical Press, 1978.

Federation of Diocesan Liturgical Commissions. *The Mystery of Faith.* Washington, D.C.: FDLC, 1981.

Fitzgerald, Timothy. "General Intercessions." *Liturgy 90* (May/June 1990): 9-12.

Gelineau, Joseph. *Learning to Celebrate.* Washington, D.C.: The Pastoral Press, 1985.

Huck, Gabe, ed., *Liturgy with Style and Grace.* Chicago: Liturgy Training Publications, 1984.

Keifer, Ralph. *To Give Thanks and Praise.* Washington, D.C.: National Association of Pastoral Musicians, 1980.

3.

LITURGY OF
THE EUCHARIST

Preparation Rites
Eucharistic Prayer
Communion Rite

Preparation Rites

Overview

The Last Supper. The liturgical structure for the eucharistic celebration hinges upon seven actions performed by Jesus at the Last Supper. The New Testament accounts tell us that toward the beginning of the meal, Christ...

    1. took bread;

    2. offered a prayer of blessing over the bread;

    3. broke the bread;

    4. distributed the bread.

Toward the conclusion of the meal, he...

    1. took a cup of wine;

    2. offered a prayer of blessing over the cup;

    3. distributed the wine.

The Early Christians. These actions, although given new meaning at the Last Supper, were commonly observed whenever the Jewish people formally gathered at table. The primitive Christian community, faithful to Christ's command "Do this in memory of me," continued to make memory of the Lord as its members also carried out these actions within a meal. At an early period, however, and for various reasons, the eucharistic actions were separated from the meal. A gradual process of ritualization and simplification apparently followed:

    1. bread and wine were taken together;

    2. one blessing was said over both elements;

3. the bread was broken;

4. the bread and wine were shared among those present.

These four steps have come to be known as the "shape of the liturgy." Even though various prayers and ceremonies, differing according to places, times, and mentalities, were added to the celebration, this fourfold pattern is the structural foundation for all ancient as well as contemporary eucharistic liturgies. In the Roman Church, the taking of bread and wine came to be known as the offertory although it is now called the preparation of the gifts. The prayer of blessing developed into the eucharistic prayer. The breaking of the bread occurs after the sign of peace and serves as a preparation for the distribution of the Eucharist.

Preparation: From Simple Action to Complex Ritual. Already in the early church the simple and functional actions of taking bread and wine were expanded and formalized. One of the earliest tasks of the deacon, for example, was to bring in the bread and wine for the celebration. Eventually the faithful brought not only these elements, but also such items as oil, wax, flowers, and food for the poor. In some areas the people deposited their gifts near the door of the church; in others, they brought them in procession to the presiding bishop who received what was necessary for the celebration with the remainder being set aside for later distribution to the needy.

In time a number of significant changes occurred: various private prayers and ceremonies were introduced; the procession gradually disappeared as the number of communicants declined; the content of the newly introduced prayers tended to anticipate the eucharistic prayer. Eventually the whole rite was understood as one of "offering" to God and generally came to be called the "offertory." In some places it was even known as the "little canon."

Reform. The post-Vatican II reform of the Mass attempted not only to simplify the rite but also to clarify its perspective.

No longer called the offertory, the rite is now known as the preparation of the altar and the gifts. Most liturgical authors hesitate to apply the word "offertory" here, not only because to avoid the problem of explaining what type of offering might be involved but also to avoid anticipating the true offering of sacrifice accomplished through the eucharistic prayer. What takes place is a preparation involving a ritual "setting apart" of gifts that are expressive of ourselves. It is an action which prepares the elements, the altar, and the people for what is to come.

Those who revised the *Order of Mass* also attempted to simplify the rite's structure. The fruit of their work is a compromise solution which eliminates or at least modifies many of the additions dating from the Middle Ages.

Structure. The rite has the following pattern.

Preparation of the altar

Procession and song

Prayer over the bread

Mingling of water and wine

Prayer over the wine

Prayer of the priest

Incensation

Washing of hands

Invitation to prayer

Prayer over the gifts

Of major importance are the procession with the song and the concluding prayer of the priest. Of lesser importance, perhaps, would be the short prayers over the bread and wine. All else is of minor significance.

Manner of Celebrating. Since the whole rite is preparatory, it should not be protracted. Presiders especially should be aware of the varying degrees of importance. The more significant elements should appear as such. The rubrics, for example, require that only the prayer over the gifts and its introduction be said aloud. The prayers of blessing over the bread and wine may on occasion be recited aloud. All other formulas are to be prayed quietly or, as the case may be, inaudibly since they are the priest's private devotional prayers. Failure to observe this distinction results in ritual leveling, i.e., making everything appear to be of equal importance.

Recommended Reading

Bishops' Committee on the Liturgy. "Notes on Eucharistic Celebration: Preparation of the Gifts." *Newsletter* 9 (July-August 1972).

Crichton, J. D. *Christian Celebration: The Mass*. London: Geoffrey Chapman, 1971.

Emminghaus, Johannes H. *The Eucharist: Essence, Form, Celebration*. Collegeville, Minnesota: The Liturgical Press, 1978.

Federation of Diocesan Liturgical Commissions. *The Mystery of Faith*. Washington, D.C.: FDLC, 1981.

Gelineau, Joseph. *Learning to Celebrate*. Washington, D.C.: The Pastoral Press, 1985.

Henchal, Michael J. *Sunday Worship in Your Parish*. West Mystic, Connecticut: Twenty-Third Publications, 1980.

Huck, Gabe, ed. *Liturgy with Style and Grace*. Chicago: Liturgy Training Publications, 1984.

Keifer, Ralph. "Preparation of the Altar and the Gifts or Offertory." *Worship* 48, no. 10 (December 1974): 595-600.

————. *To Give Thanks and Praise*. Washington, D.C.: National Association of Pastoral Musicians, 1980.

Preparation of the Altar

General Instruction of the Roman Missal

49. At the beginning of the Liturgy of the Eucharist the gifts, which will become Christ's body and blood, are brought to the altar.

First the altar, the Lord's table, which is the center of the whole eucharistic liturgy, is prepared: the

corporal, purificator, missal, and the chalice are
placed on it (unless the chalice is prepared at a side
table)....

100. The servers place the corporal, purificator,
chalice, and missal on the altar.

Setting the Table. This is a functional action to be attended to as
quickly as possible. Till this time the altar table has been bare
except, perhaps, for the candles. The deacon or a server places
upon it the corporal (table cloth), purificator (napkin), chalice
(drinking cup), and the Sacramentary. There is no reason why the
presider must come to the altar at this point. The preparation of
the altar is a ministerial and not a presidential task.

Procession and Song

General Instruction of the Roman Missal

49. The gifts are then brought forward. It is desirable
for the faithful to present the bread and wine, which
are accepted by the priest or deacon at a convenient
place. The gifts are placed on the altar to the
accompaniment of the prescribed texts. Even though
the faithful no longer, as in the past, bring the bread
and wine for the liturgy from their homes, the rite of
carrying up the gifts retains the same spiritual value
and meaning.

This is also the time to receive money or other
gifts for the church or the poor brought by the
faithful or collected at Mass. These are to be put in a
suitable place but not on the altar.

50. The procession bringing the gifts is accompanied
by the presentation song, which continues at least
until the gifts have been placed on the altar. The
rules for this song are the same as those for the
entrance song (no. 26). If it is not sung, the
presentation antiphon is omitted.

Collection. It is an excellent sign if the presider and other ministers in the sanctuary wait till the gifts are collected. In this way all the gifts, including monetary offerings, can be brought up in the procession.

A sufficient number of ushers is required if the collection is not to be prolonged. Collection plates or baskets passed hand to hand not only are less awkward but also more actively involve everyone in the act of presenting. Second collections are thereby easily facilitated since another set of receptacles can be immediately started. It says much if the ministers in the sanctuary also contribute their monetary offerings.

Some communities designate a portion of each collection or have special collections for a purpose other than parish maintenance since the gifts are, according to the *General Instruction*, "for the church or the poor" (49). In such a case a petition may be formulated in the general intercessions to make the community aware of the particular need for which some of the money will be used.

In other parishes a large, attractive basket is located in the church vestibule. The members of the assembly are encouraged to bring with them each Sunday such items as nonperishable food, used clothing in good condition, and the like to place in the basket which is brought to the altar in the procession. During the week the goods are distributed by parish members to the needy.

Procession. The size of the procession should be proportionate to the character of the celebration. Individual parish members as well as families can be requested to volunteer for particular liturgies. Every effort should be made to represent all segments of the community (e.g., the separated and divorced, widows and widowers, single persons, members of the various ethnic groups, the handicapped, etc.) in obtaining volunteers. Advance planning is so important here to avoid plucking persons from the pews at the last moment.

The primary symbols in the procession are the bread and the wine. Water, being an accessory, is not presented, nor is the chalice. Proliferation is avoided in larger assemblies when one large breadplate and, if communion will be distributed under both forms, a large flagon are used. In addition to the monetary offerings, which are placed in an attractive receptacle, other symbolic gifts appropriate to the occasion may be presented. These, however, should never overwhelm the primacy of the bread and wine.

The procession is a symbolic action and, as such, should be more than a visually impoverished walk of a few steps from a table placed near the front of the building. Its participants, to avoid needless delay, should be in position before the ushers finish the collection. If there is no collection, care should be taken that the procession, meant to be seen, does not begin till all are seated after the general intercessions. A cross bearer and acolytes may lead the participants and thereby ensure a moderate pace of movement. The presider, accompanied by one or two ministers, receives the bread and wine. A friendly word and gesture are not inappropriate. The elements for the Eucharist are placed upon the altar. The monetary gifts should not be spirited off to the sacristy since they, like the bread and wine, are expressive of our lives. Rather, they as well as any other appropriate gifts, are placed in a fitting location near the altar.

Song and Silence. The *General Instruction* suggests but does not require that song accompany the procession.

To provide a respite from the high degree of involvement entailed by the Liturgy of the Word, many communities use these moments of the celebration as a time for quiet and reflection. The assembly is offered a breathing space, an opportunity for silent prayer, perhaps sustained by soft instrumental music. This approach not only respects the secondary character of this period of preparation but also provides a calm transition to the eucharistic prayer which is the very heart of the Liturgy of the Eucharist.

If there is to be song, many options are possible. To mention just a few:

1. instrumental music during the collection, a
     short hymn to accompany the procession, a
     very brief choir piece during the rest of the rite;

2. a choir selection during the collection,
   instrumental music during the procession,
   silence during the remainder of the rite;

3. silence during the collection, a short hymn
   during the procession, silence during the rest
   of the rite.

Much variety is possible and, taking into account the overall flow
of the celebration, is to be encouraged. Yet whatever options are
used, they should not prolong the rite.

Choosing Texts. Lyrics expressing joy and praise help create an
atmosphere within which the action takes place. Seasonal texts
are appropriate. Also suitable are texts articulating the "spirit"
of the action. To be avoided, however, are lyrics which tend to
anticipate the eucharistic prayer, e.g., "Accept, Almighty
Father," "Accept the Gifts We Offer," and the like.

Recommended Reading

Bishops' Committee on the Liturgy. *Music in Catholic Worship*, 71. Washington, D.C.: USCC, 1983.

Deiss, Lucien. *Spirit and Song of the New Liturgy*. Cincinnati: World Library of Sacred Music, 1976.

Emminghaus, Johannes H. *The Eucharist: Essence, Form, Celebration*. Collegeville, Minnesota: The Liturgical Press, 1978.

Federation of Diocesan Liturgical Commissions. *The Mystery of Faith*. Washington, D.C.: FDLC, 1981.

Hovda, Robert. "Money or Gifts for the Poor and the Church." *Worship* 59, no. 1 (January 1985): 65-71.

Prayers over the Bread and Wine

General Instruction of the Roman Missal

102. At the altar the priest receives the paten with the
bread from a minister. With both hands he holds it
slightly raised above the altar and says the

accompanying prayer. Then he places the paten with the bread on the corporal.

103. He returns to the middle of the altar, takes the chalice, raises it a little with both hands, and says the appointed prayer. Then he places the chalice on the corporal and may cover it with a pall.

Not a Gesture of Offering. The *General Instruction* calls for the presider to hold the paten or chalice "slightly" or "a little" above the altar. The directive is significant for this is not a gesture of offering. Rather, it is one of pointing out, of showing to the people, of focusing attention upon the bread and wine.

Praise of God. Although of recent composition, these prayers are very similar to the blessing formulas characteristic of Judaism and used by Christ during the Last Supper. These prayers praise God's holiness and goodness. It is God, not the bread and wine, that is blessed. In this context, we praise God because we have been created to work with God in the continuing work of creation. Bread and wine are the symbols of our life and labor on earth. They will be transformed into a new level of existence as they become our "bread of life" and our "spiritual drink."

Order of Preference. The *Order of Mass* seems to give this order of preference for the manner of reciting these prayers:

1. The presiding priest says the prayer in a low voice if there is singing;

2. if there is no music or singing, he says the text quietly; or

3. he may say it aloud;

4. if there is no song and if the priest says the formula aloud, the people may give the acclamation at the end.

When the prayers are said aloud, this should be done simply, without the expansiveness used, for example, during the eucharistic prayer. If the people give the acclamation, it is a good sign if the priest does not place the paten and chalice back upon the altar till all have given the response.

Recommended Reading

Bishops' Committee on the Liturgy. "Notes on Eucharistic Celebration: Preparation of the Gifts." *Newsletter* 8 (July-August 1972).

Emminghaus, Johannes H. *The Eucharist: Essence, Form, Celebration.* Collegeville, Minnesota: The Liturgical Press, 1978.

Federation of Diocesan Liturgical Commissions. *The Mystery of Faith.* Washington, D.C.: FDLC, 1981.

Mingling of Water and Wine

General Instruction of the Roman Missal

103. Next, as a minister presents the cruets, the priest stands at the side of the altar and pours wine and a little water into the chalice, saying the accompanying prayer softly....

Functional Gesture to Symbolic Meaning. Before saying the prayer of blessing over the wine, the priest pours a little water into the cup. This action derives from early cultures where the strong wine was often diluted before use so that it would be less potent. The custom continued in Christian liturgical practice. In the East, this action came to represent the two natures united in Christ; in the West, it was the union of Christ with his people or, in some areas, the water and blood flowing from the side of the crucified Christ which were understood. During the early Middle Ages, a text, namely a modification of a Christmas oration, was added to the Roman Mass.

Recent History. The recent history of the mingling rite is somewhat strange. The redactors of the *Order of Mass* proposed that the rite be maintained but without any accompanying prayer. The 1967 Synod of Bishops, recognizing that most Catholics fail to understand the meaning of the gesture, requested that a formula accompany the prayer. This was done. However, the prayer is to be said quietly. The rite is certainly not significant, and the prayer ranks among the private texts of the priest.

Some Practicalities. The water and wine need not be prepared at the altar, as it may also be done on a side table. (Refer to the *General Instruction*, 133, 147.) If a deacon is assisting, he prepares the chalice with a little water and hands it to the presider. Otherwise, the priest himself places the wine and water in the chalice. It should be noted that it is a "little water" which is added to the wine and not a "few drops" as formerly.

Prayer of the Priest

General Instruction of the Roman Missal

104. The priest bows and says softly the prayer, *Lord God, we ask you to receive.*

Retaining a Medieval Addition. This prayer is reminiscent of the numerous "apologies" found in the medieval Mass whereby the priest professed his personal sentiments of sinfulness and the need for pardon. The present text, added to the Mass in Middle Ages, is taken from the Book of Daniel (3:39-40). A number of Protestant liturgies have a corresponding formula known as the "Prayer of Humble Access." According to the translation of the *General Instruction* appearing in the most recent editions of the Sacramentary, the prayer of the priest is prayed inaudibly.

Incensation

General Instruction of the Roman Missal

51. The gifts on the altar and the altar itself may be incensed. This is a symbol of the Church's offering

and prayer going up to God. Afterward the deacon or
other minister may incense the priest and people.

Meaning. This incensation, the most ancient of those in the
Roman Mass, symbolizes the spirit of prayer with which the gifts
will be offered in the eucharistic prayer. All are to join themselves
and their prayers to the bread and the wine.

Some Practicalities. If the altar has been incensed at the beginning of the celebration, it might be well here to incense only the
gifts, the ministers, and the people. Duplication is thereby
avoided. The incense is placed in the censer and blessed with the
sign of the cross. The formerly prescribed series of crosses and
circles was deliberately eliminated from the *Order of Mass*. The
gifts are incensed with three swings of the censer, and the altar
as at the beginning of the liturgy.

Washing of Hands

General Instruction of the Roman Missal

52. The priest then washes his hands as an expression
of his desire to be cleansed within.

106. After the prayer, *Lord God, we ask you to receive*,
or after the incensation, the priest washes his hands
at the side of the altar and softly says the prescribed
prayer as a minister pours the water.

Origins. The history of the Roman Mass has known various
washings of the hands. Sometimes this was required for practical
reasons as, for example, when the gifts received from the faithful
might have included items other than bread and wine. In some
regions the priest washed his hands as a symbol of internal
purification and separation from the everyday world. Eventually,
this gesture was accompanied by several verses of Psalm 26, which
verbalized the need for spiritual cleansing.

Recent History. The artisans of the *Order of Mass* were of various opinions regarding this rite. At any rate, they eventually decided to retain it but without any accompanying formula. In 1967 the Synod of Bishops requested that a text be added. Accordingly, verse four of Psalm 51 was added, but, as a private formula, it is recited softly.

Some Details. If an action is to be performed, it should be carried out in a meaningful manner. Thus it is most appropriate that a real towel as well as an attractive pitcher of water and basin be used. The water is to be poured over the hands of the priest and not merely over his fingers as formerly.

Prayer over the Gifts and Its Invitation

General Instruction of the Roman Missal

107. The priest returns to the center and, facing the people and extending then joining his hands, pronounces the invitation: *Pray, brothers and sisters.* After the people's response, he says the prayer over the gifts with his hands outstretched. At the end the people make the acclamation: *Amen.*

32. The prayer over the gifts and the prayer after communion end with the shorter conclusion, namely:
  — if the prayer is directed to the Father: *We ask this (Grant this) through Christ our Lord;*
  — if it is directed to the Father, but the Son is mentioned at the end: *Who lives and reigns with you for ever and ever;*
  — if it is directed to the Son: *You live and reign for ever and ever.*

Partially Restoring an Ancient Tradition. For many centuries a single prayer was recited by the priest over the bread and wine received from the people, namely, the "prayer over the gifts." Spoken aloud, it eventually came to be prayed silently and consequently was termed the "secret." The text, like that of the opening prayer, was preceded by an introduction inviting the assembly to prayer silently. But by the Middle Ages, a standardized and expanded form of the invitation developed, i.e., "Pray, brethren..." together with a spoken response, i.e., "May the Lord..." which replaced the silent prayer of all. The *Order of Mass*, perhaps for reasons of pious tradition, has retained this structure, but has also restored the prayer's original title and public manner of recitation.

Content of the Prayer. Looking forward to the eucharistic prayer, the priest, often in very terse form, requests that the gifts may be accepted by the Father and may bring forth spiritual fruits for the people who have united themselves to them.

Some Reminders. The priest may creatively adapt the invitation to circumstances and occasions. He visibly respects the people's role by waiting till the conclusion of the response before turning to the Sacramentary to locate the page for the prayer over the gifts. If, as is customary in the United States, the people are to stand for this oration, time must be allotted so that all can rise and come to attentiveness before the priest begins. The text, although prayed with somewhat the same expansiveness as the opening prayer, ends with the short conclusion as indicated in the *General Instruction*, 32.

Concelebration. After the prayer over the gifts the concelebrants come to the altar. They...

> should remain out of the way of the deacon and other
> ministers in such a way that the people are able to
> see the rite clearly. This means that they should place
> themselves at least several feet from the altar for the
> altar is designed and constructed for the action of a
> community and the functioning of a single priest —
> not concelebrants (Bishops' Committee on the
> Liturgy, *Eucharistic Concelebration*, Study Text 5,
> [Washington, D.C.: USCC, 1978], 7).

Recommended Reading

Emminghaus, Johannes H. *The Eucharist: Essence, Form, Celebration*. Collegeville, Minnesota: The Liturgical Press, 1978.

Federation of Diocesan Liturgical Commissions. *The Mystery of Faith*. Washington, D.C.: FDLC, 1981.

Eucharistic Prayer

Overview

Jewish Roots. The eucharistic prayer, like so many elements of Christian worship, originated in Jewish cultic life, especially in a type of literary genre or prayer known as the *berakah*. Often used by the Jewish people on both public and private occasions, prayers of this kind were said by Jesus at the Last Supper, i.e. a short formula over the bread and a longer formula over the wine as was customary in Jewish meal practice.

Although assuming various forms, the *berakah* prayer contains four elements: exclamation, memorial, petition, and doxology.

> **1. Exclamation.** The prayer begins with an exclamation, a proclamatory statement of admiration and awe prompted by a remembrance of God's good deeds. Thus the predominant motif is one of praise and thanksgiving. God's marvelous deeds are blessed and praised on behalf of a people who have experienced these works.

> **2. Memorial or Remembrance.** The motive for praise is then articulated. God is glorified not only for previous accomplishments but also for present actions on behalf of the people. Ever faithful to the covenant, God continues to act. God's wonderful works unfailingly endure and we still experience them. It was especially at Passover that the Jews were conscious of this religious psychology. At this time, the Exodus event was reactualized, made present, and so experienced by the participants of the meal that the father of the family could declare: "In every generation let

each man look on himself as if he came forth
out of Egypt....It was not only our fathers that
the Holy One redeemed, but us as well did he
redeem along with them."

3. Supplication. God is requested to extend his
assistance and protection to the days ahead.
The works of creation and redemption are to
continue and be ultimately fulfilled in the
establishment of the kingdom.

4. Doxology. The prayer concludes with a short
hymn or statement of praise.

Christian Adaptation. The prototype of the eucharistic prayer is,
as already mentioned, the Jewish *berakah*, specifically the prayer
pronounced toward the end of the meal over the wine. But
already at an early period the formula was fashioned to express
the Christian community's understanding of itself, its own experience of God's wonderful deeds, especially those manifested in
the Lord Jesus. Terminology and thought patterns began to take
on a Christian perspective. During the first centuries, the bishop,
although following the inherited general model, improvised this
prayer of praise over the bread and wine. By the end of the fourth
century, however, fixed formulas became the rule. These would
assume various literary and structural characteristics according
to diverse geographical centers of church leadership. Whereas
the East always possessed a great variety of such prayers, such
was not the case at Rome.

Designations. Throughout history a number of names have been
applied to the prayer. For example, the Roman Church long
referred to it as the "canon," from the Greek meaning "measur-
ing-rod" or "rule." Originally this word formed part of the phrase
canon actionis gratiarum, i.e., the "norm for the thanksgiving."
Today the Roman liturgy uses another term, one which also has
historical roots, namely the *prex eucharista*, i.e., "eucharistic
prayer." In the East the prayer is called the *anaphora*, a Greek
word meaning an offering or an elevation of the heart.

Nature. The *General Instruction* (54) speaks of the eucharistic prayer as being the "center and summit of the entire celebration" by which the assembly "joins itself to Christ in acknowledging the great things God has done and in offering the sacrifice." It is *the* prayer of "thanksgiving and sanctification." As such, the prayer recalls God's past works, articulates God's present activity on our behalf, and evokes a future that surpasses our hopes and dreams. Developing its themes in broad strokes and couched in a language which is formal, lyrical, and elevated, the prayer is a summary of what it means to celebrate the Eucharist together. It is the whole assembly's prayer although proclaimed by the priest acting in the name of all. It is a prayer through which the eucharistic elements are transformed into Christ's body and blood. Its ultimate end is the transformation of the whole assembly.

Recommended Reading

Bishops' Committee on the Liturgy. *Music in Catholic Worship*, 47. Washington, D.C.: USCC, 1983.

Bouyer, Louis. *Eucharist: Theology and Spirituality of the Eucharistic Prayer.* Trans. by Charles Underhill Quinn. Notre Dame: University of Notre Dame Press, 1968.

Ciferni, Andrew D., and Elizabeth Hoffman. "The Eucharistic Prayer — Center and Summit?" *Liturgy 90* (May/June 1992).

Deiss, Lucien. *Spirit and Song of the New Liturgy.* Cincinnati: World Library of Sacred Music, 1976.

Federation of Diocesan Liturgical Commissions. *The Mystery of Faith.* Washington, D.C.: FDLC, 1981.

Funk, Virgil, ed., *Music in Catholic Worship: The NPM Commentary.* Washington, D.C.: National Association of Pastoral Musicians, 1982.

Gelineau, Joseph. *Learning to Celebrate.* Washington, D.C.: The Pastoral Press, 1985.

————. *The Eucharistic Prayer: Praise of the Whole Assembly.* Washington, D.C.: The Pastoral Press, 1985.

Henchal, Michael. *Sunday Worship in Your Parish.* West Mystic, Connecticut: Twenty-Third Publications, 1980.

Huck, Gabe. *Preaching about the Mass.* Chicago: Liturgy Training Publications, 1992.

Huck, Gabe, ed., *Liturgy with Style and Grace*. Chicago: Liturgy Training Publications, 1984.

Keifer, Ralph. *To Give Thanks and Praise*. Washington, D.C.: National Association of Pastoral Musicians, 1980.

Ligier, Louis. "From the Last Supper to the Eucharist." In *The New Liturgy: A Comprehensive Introduction*. Ed. by Lancelot Sheppard. London: Longman & Todd, 1970.

Smolarski, Dennis C. *Eucharistica: A Study of the Eucharistic Prayer*. Ramsey, New Jersey: Paulist Press, 1982.

Roman Canon

Origins and Development. For centuries the Roman rite knew but one eucharistic prayer, called the Roman canon. Most probably written in Latin, its text goes back to the time of Pope Damasus I (366-384) and was known by Saint Ambrose (c. 339-397). The prayer underwent various elaborations until stabilized and edited by Pope Gregory I (590-604). Since then, only a few modifications have occurred, e.g., the insertion of "through Christ our Lord. Amen" at four places within the text, and the 1962 addition by Pope John XXIII of St. Joseph's name to the list of saints.

Need for Reform. With the introduction of the vernacular, certain weaknesses of the canon became more and more apparent: its length, its numerous repetitions (e.g. two sets of intercessory prayers, a double listing of the saints), and its lack of structural cohesiveness. Various reform projects were undertaken, but it was eventually realized that no substantial modifications of the text could take place without great damage to the prayer itself.

Solution. The problem was resolved by retaining the canon without major modifications and by issuing other eucharistic prayers to be used along with the traditional formula. This solution not only respects the venerable character and merits of the canon, but also offers the Roman Church a variety of prayers for expressing the inexhaustible richness of the eucharistic mystery.

Roman Canon Today. Now known as Eucharistic Prayer I, the canon may be slightly altered at the discretion of the presider. For instance, he need not mention all the names included in the listings of the saints. Furthermore, the "through Christ our Lord. Amen" is now optional since the prayer is one prayer and consequently should not be segmented. The text can be used at any time, but it is especially appropriate for those days having a proper *Communicantes* or *Hanc igitur*, e.g., Christmas and its octave, Epiphany, Holy Thursday, from the Easter Vigil till the Second Sunday of Easter inclusive, Ascension, and Pentecost. It is also suitable on Sundays and on the feasts of those saints mentioned in its commemorations.

Recommended Reading

Emminghaus, Johannes H. *The Eucharist: Essence, Form, Celebration.* Collegeville, Minnesota: The Liturgical Press, 1978.

Vagaggini, Cipriano. *The Canon of the Mass and Liturgical Reform.* New York: Alba House, 1967.

Three New Eucharistic Prayers

In 1968, three new eucharistic prayers for use in the Roman liturgy appeared.

Eucharistic Prayer II. This formula is in substance based on one of the most ancient eucharistic texts that has come down to us, that found in the third century work known as the *Apostolic Tradition* written by Hippolytus of Rome. The early model has been adapted for present use by the addition of certain elements, e.g., a Sanctus, an invocation of the Holy Spirit, intercessory prayers. Although the text has its proper preface, others might be substituted, especially those recalling the mystery of salvation. Being the shortest and most concise of all the new prayers, it is intended not for Sundays but for those weekdays and special occasions when a more simplified form might be desired.

LITURGY OF THE EUCHARIST

Eucharistic Prayer III. This prayer, midway in length between Eucharistic Prayers II and IV, draws from or is inspired by various eucharistic prayers found in liturgies of the West and East. It may be used with any of the prefaces found in the Sacramentary.

Eucharistic Prayer IV. The longest of the three new prayers, the text is characterized by a highly theological content developed by references to many biblical themes. As such, it is especially appropriate for groups possessing a good scriptural understanding. Since the prayer has a proper preface which is integral to the development of the text, other prefaces are not to be used. Some suggest that the prayer is best used on days when there is no profession of faith since, otherwise, many themes would be repeated.

Recommended Reading

Botte, Bernard. "The Short Anaphora." In *The New Liturgy: A Comprehensive Introduction*. Ed. by Lancelot Sheppard. London: Longman & Todd, 1970.

Bouyer, Louis. "The Third Eucharist Prayer." In *The New Liturgy: A Comprehensive Introduction*. Ed. by Lancelot Sheppard. London: Longman & Todd, 1970.

Emminghaus, Johannes H. *The Eucharist: Essence, Form, Celebration*. Collegeville, Minnesota: The Liturgical Press, 1978.

Gelineau, Joseph. "The Fourth Eucharist Prayer." In *New Liturgy: A Comprehensive Introduction*. Ed. by Lancelot Sheppard. London: Longman & Todd, 1970.

Kavanagh, Aidan. "Thoughts on the New Eucharistic Prayers." *Worship* 43, no. 1 (January 1969): 2-12.

Soubigou, Louis. *A Commentary on the Prefaces and the Eucharistic Prayers of the Roman Missal*. Trans. by John A. Otto. Collegeville, Minnesota: The Liturgical Press, 1971.

Other Eucharistic Prayers

In 1974, five other eucharistic prayers were authorized for use in the Roman Church. At the request of several bishops and episcopal conferences, three prayers were prepared for Masses with Children; two others were issued for use during the Holy

Year and afterwards when reconciliation would be the theme of the celebration. Their texts are incorporated only in editions of the Sacramentary printed after August 1985. The booklet, *Eucharistic Prayers for Masses of Reconciliation,* is obtainable from the Publications Office of the United States Catholic Conference.

Individual episcopal conferences can submit for the approval of the Holy See compositions for use within their own countries. So far, no such compositions have been approved for the United States.

Eucharistic Prayers for Children. These prayers may be used during Masses for children only when the majority of the participants are children. All three formularies are characterized by their use of acclamations. Prayer I is a very simple and is marked by a very concrete imagery. About half of the text is devoted to the preface which is punctuated by acclamatory strophes of the Sanctus. Prayer II has an increased number of acclamations, twelve in all, comprising some 25 percent of the text. Prayer III allows for seasonal and occasional inserts at three places. The printed text offer samples for the Easter season; conferences of bishops may compose others. The text is quite unusual since it lacks an explicit consecratory invocation of the Holy Spirit.

Eucharistic Prayers for Masses of Reconciliation. Both prayers may be used when the mystery of reconciliation is a special theme of the celebration. Prayer I develops this theme under such images as covenant, friendship, fullness of joy, new creation, and unity. Prayer II places special emphasis upon the meal as the biblical image of reconciliation.

Recommended Reading

International Committee on English in the Liturgy. "Eucharistic Prayers for Children." *Pastoral Music* 10, no. 2 (December-January 1986): 13-14.

Ryan, John Barry. *The Eucharistic Prayer: A Study in Contemporary Theology.* New York: Paulist Press, 1974.

Proclamation

Tradition: A Need, An Answer. There exist three ancient traditions in the church which govern the proclamation of the eucharistic prayer. The first, although apparently admitting some very rare exceptions, is that the proclamation of the prayer is reserved to an ordained minister, in particular, the bishop or priest. Another tradition is that this prayer is ordinarily proclaimed by one person alone. This, for example, was the early practice at Rome, even when many priests or bishops were present and "concelebrating." It has always remained such in the East. Although verbal concelebration was introduced into the West during the High Middle Ages, the ancient usage is that only one ordained person functions as the leader or spokesman for the assembly in articulating the praise over the bread and wine. A third tradition, found in both East and West, is that the whole community demonstrates its participation in the prayer by means of various acclamations. The use of such acclamatory expressions has been restored and highlighted in our present eucharistic prayers.

Today, however, some communities experience a need to express more fully the involvement of all present. Accordingly, the practice has developed in a few parishes whereby everyone joins the ordained minister in proclaiming the eucharistic prayer, either in its totality or in part, e.g., the concluding doxology, "Through him...."

Good intentions notwithstanding, such a practice is just poor liturgy. It runs counter to the most ancient tradition of the church. It overlooks the distinction of liturgical roles. It disregards the origin of the eucharistic prayer, i.e., the Jewish meal prayer or *berakah* which was prayed in the name of all by the head of the family. It is as logical as having all present read aloud the scriptural readings. The September 1970 *Instruction on the Constitution on the Liturgy* (4) is most explicit:

> The eucharistic prayer more than any other part of
> the Mass, is by reason of his office, the prayer of the
> priest alone. Recitation of any part by a lesser

minister, the assembly, or any individual is forbidden. Such a course conflicts with the hierarchic character of the liturgy in which all are to do all but only those parts belonging to them. The priest alone, therefore, is to recite the entire eucharistic prayer.

A more creative and certainly legitimate practice is to insert short acclamations sung by the assembly throughout the eucharistic prayer. Their recurring use upholds and encourages the voice of the presider yet does not supplant his unique role. These should be true acclamations of praise and thanksgiving which thus give a cohesive motif to the prayer's development. Such an approach, traditional in the Coptic and Armenian liturgies, is found in the eucharistic prayers for children.

Presider and Assembly. Being the most solemn speech of the Mass, the eucharistic prayer places unique demands upon both presider and assembly. Obviously, the text is to be proclaimed in a loud and clear voice. The words are to stand alone, unaccompanied by any instrumental background. The prayer is a public prayer and is to appear as such through the presider's vocal energy, pace of delivery, and bodily expression.

Although an expression of praise addressed to the Father, the prayer involves the whole assembly. Expansive gestures, eye contact, and a general awareness of the assembly help draw all present into what is and what should appear to be a statement springing from the faith of the whole community. For its part, the assembly not only listens attentively but also demonstrates its participation through various acclamations which are integral to the prayer.

The presider, after the prayer over the gifts, does well to pause a moment or two before the preface so that the assembly might experience that something new and important is about to begin. He may also give a few words of introduction.

Recommended Reading

Deiss, Lucien. *Spirit and Song of the New Liturgy*. Cincinnati: World Library of Sacred Music, 1976.

Structure

Although the eucharistic prayer is essentially a unified formula, several structural elements can be identified as forming this whole. These elements or segments are found in the recently composed Roman eucharistic prayers as well as in the vast majority of ancient eucharistic formulas found in both East and West. These textual segments explicitly highlight themes which permeate the whole prayer and thus exist in relationship one to another. They can be identified as:

> Thanksgiving (preface)
>
> Acclamation (Sanctus)
>
> Epiclesis (invocation of the Holy Spirit)
>
> Narrative of the institution and consecration
>
> Anamnesis ("memorial" of the passion and of the whole mystery of Christ)
>
> Prayer that the offering be received
>
> Intercessions and commemorations
>
> Concluding Doxology

Preface

General Instruction of the Roman Missal

55. The chief elements of the eucharistic prayer are these:

a. Thanksgiving (expressed especially in the preface): in the name of the entire people of God, the priest praises the Father and gives thanks to him for the whole work of salvation or for some special aspect of it that corresponds to the day, feast, or season.

Statement of Praise and Its Motive. The preface, a word whose meaning here is not one of "introduction" but rather "proclamation" or "speaking out," begins with a dialogue inviting the whole assembly to enter into the action of the eucharistic prayer. The presider, following the pattern of the Jewish *berakah*, then praises and thanks the Father for the benefits bestowed upon God's people, especially for the gifts of creation and redemption. At times this laudatory statement is couched in terms appropriate to the season or the feast being celebrated.

Variety of Texts. The Sacramentary provides eighty texts and thus resembles certain ancient liturgical books which offered a great variety of such formulas. Prefaces are provided for:

- Advent (2)

- Christmas (3)

- Epiphany; Baptism of the Lord; Lent (4)

- Sundays of Lent (5)

- Passion of the Lord (3)

- Priesthood (Chrism Mass); Easter (5)

- Ascension; Sacred Heart; Triumph of the Cross; Holy Eucharist (2)

- Presentation of the Lord; Transfiguration; Christ the King; Dedication of a Church (2)

- Holy Spirit (2)

- Blessed Virgin Mary (2)

- Immaculate Conception; Assumption; Angels; St. John the Baptist; St. Joseph; St. Peter and St. Paul; Apostles (2)

- Martyrs; Pastors; Virgins and Religious; Holy Men and Women (2)

- All Saints; Marriage (3)

- Religious Profession; Christian Unity; Christian Death (2)

In the United States prefaces are provided for:

- Independence Day and Other Civic Observances (2)

- Thanksgiving Day.

Liturgy planners should study the content and suggested uses for these texts to determine which best correspond to the occasion and the assembly. For example, the preface for Thanksgiving Day with its statement that "...our fathers...came to this land...into a place of promise and hope..." would certainly be offensive to many members of the community.

Praise in Song. As the solemn beginning of the eucharistic prayer, the preface is most appropriately sung. Because of their beauty and variety, melodic settings are preferable to recto-tono render-ings. Chant settings for the prefaces as well as the texts for the four eucharistic prayers are given in the Sacramentary. Jan Kern has most skillfully set the prefaces to music in *Eighty-Six Prefaces from the Roman Missal* (GIA Publications, 1973).

Recommended Reading

Emminghaus, Johannes H. *The Eucharist: Essence, Form, Celebration*. Col-legeville, Minnesota: The Liturgical Press, 1978.

Federation of Diocesan Liturgical Commissions. *The Mystery of Faith*. Wash-ington, D.C.: FDLC, 1981.

Gelineau, Joseph. *Learning to Celebrate*. Washington, D.C.: The Pastoral Press, 1985.

Jarrell, Stephen T. *Guide to the Sacramentary*. Chicago: Liturgy Training Publications, 1983.

Rose, Andre. "The New Prefaces." In *The New Liturgy: A Comprehensive Introduction*. Ed. by Lancelot Sheppard. London: Longman & Todd, 1970.

Soubigou, Louis. *A Commentary on the Prefaces and the Eucharistic Prayers of the Roman Missal.* Trans. by John A. Otto. Collegeville, Minnesota: The Liturgical Press, 1971.

"Holy, Holy, Holy Lord"

General Instruction of the Roman Missal

55b. Acclamation: joining with the angels, the congregation sings or recites the *Sanctus*. This acclamation is an intrinsic part of the eucharistic prayer and all the people join with the priest in singing or reciting it.

Another Legacy from Judaism. The "Holy, Holy, Holy Lord" is a text inspired by the vision of Isaiah (6:2-3). Appearing at an early age in the eucharistic prayer, the acclamation probably entered the liturgy by way of the synagogue morning service which was very familiar to many members of the post-apostolic community. Since the preface traditionally concludes by evoking the angels who praise God, the Sanctus is given a natural link with the preface itself. The "Blessed is he..." is the acclamation used by the people as they greeted Christ on Passion Sunday (Matthew 21:9). It was joined to the Sanctus as early as the sixth century.

Sung by All. From the very beginning the Sanctus was looked upon as an acclamation or hymn to be sung by all. It is therefore not sung by the choir alone. Every parish can learn at least two or three good congregational settings of this acclamation whose music should be forceful and acclamatory.

A Reminder for Pastoral Musicians. Since the preface leads into the "Holy, Holy...," care must be taken that the acclamation begins immediately after the presider's concluding words. The rhythmic flow of the celebration is thereby preserved. Often a single introductory note suffices when the setting is well-known.

A Reminder for Presiders. After the "Holy, Holy...," the priest, if the people will be kneeling during the remainder of the eucharistic prayer, should pause before continuing. This allows the noise caused by many people changing posture to subside.

Recommended Reading

Bishops' Committee on the Liturgy. *Music in Catholic Worship*, 56. Washington, D.C.: USCC, 1983.

Deiss, Lucien. *Spirit and Song of the New Liturgy*. Cincinnati: World Library of Sacred Music, 1976.

Emminghaus, Johannes H. *Eucharist: Essence, Form, Celebration*. Collegeville, Minnesota: The Liturgical Press, 1978.

Federation of Diocesan Liturgical Commissions. *The Mystery of Faith*. Washington, D.C.: FDLC, 1981.

Gelineau, Joseph. *Learning to Celebrate*. Washington, D.C.: The Pastoral Press, 1985.

Epiclesis

General Instruction of the Roman Missal

55c. Epiclesis: in special invocations the Church calls on God's power and asks that the gifts offered by human hands be consecrated, that is, become Christ's body and blood, and that the victim to be received in communion be the source of salvation for those who will partake.

A Technical Word. The Greek word *epiclesis* means "invocation," here an invocation that the Spirit, the power of God, may come and transform both the bread and the wine as well as the whole community.

Two Traditions. The churches of the East have placed great emphasis upon invoking the Holy Spirit during the Eucharist. The West, however, has emphasized the words of institution or consecration. Although both approaches have merit, we should beware of unduly segmenting the nature of the eucharistic prayer. Recent theological reflection highlights the unitive character of the prayer and recalls that the whole prayer is consecratory.

A Double Invocation. Although the Roman Canon (Eucharistic Prayer I) has no explicit invocation of the Spirit, the recently composed eucharistic prayers usually contain a double request that the Spirit come.

The first petition occurs before the institution narrative and asks that the Spirit may come to "make holy" or "sanctify" the offerings so that they "become" or are "changed into" the Lord's body and blood.

The second, found toward the conclusion of the eucharistic prayer, requests that the assembly attain that unity of the Holy Spirit which is to be characteristic of the Body of Christ.

The Gesture. During the first epiclesis, the presiding priest imposes hands over the bread and wine as he begins the petition. This gesture should be performed with care and solemnity. It is the ancient and primary symbol of invoking the Spirit. The sign of the cross which follows is secondary. On occasions of concelebration the priests extend their hands or at least their right hands toward the gifts until the presider has made the sign of the cross.

Recommended Reading

Crichton, J. D. *Christian Celebration: The Mass*. London: Geoffrey Chapman, 1971.

Federation of Diocesan Liturgical Commissions. *The Mystery of Faith*. Washington, D.C.: FDLC, 1981.

Institution Narrative

General Instruction of the Roman Missal

55d. Institution narrative and consecration: in the words and actions of Christ, that sacrifice is celebrated which he himself instituted at the Last Supper, when, under the appearances of bread and wine, he offered his body and blood, gave them to his apostles to eat and drink, then commanded that they carry on this mystery.

A Microcosm. The narrative of our Lord's actions and words at the Last Supper is found in almost every eucharistic prayer that has come down to us since the early church. Although the whole eucharistic celebration is a ritual remembrance of what Christ said and did in the upper room, the institution narrative is a microcosm of this event. It is crucial to the eucharistic prayer, which makes present not only Christ's body and blood but also the totality of the mystery of Christ's death, resurrection, and glorification.

The Text. In addition to the four biblical accounts of the institution, over eighty other institution accounts used in various eucharistic prayers have come down to us. Although these formulas attempt to keep their wording close to the scriptural versions, numerous variations as well as slight embellishments, e.g., the incorporation of acclamations by the assembly, are found. In our present Roman compositions, the narrative section, i.e., "On the night...", differs from prayer to prayer while the words of Jesus, i.e., "Take this, all of you...," remain the same.

Reminders for the Presider. The priest should remember that this section is narrative in style and accordingly might be proclaimed in a manner different from that used for the preceding and following sections. The consecrated bread and wine are raised "a little above the altar." This is to show the body and blood to all present and is not a gesture of offering. A genuflection is made both after the words over the bread and those over the wine.

The practice whereby some priests break the bread at the words "He broke the bread" betrays a basic misunderstanding of the overall shape of the eucharistic liturgy. This gesture, imitating that of Christ, occurs previous to the distribution of the Eucharist, i.e., during the singing of the Lamb of God.

Concelebration.

> During the narrative of the institution, each
> concelebrant may extend his right hand toward the
> host and chalice. The form and style of such gestures
> should be agreed upon beforehand. All bow

profoundly when the celebrant genuflects after each consecration (Bishops' Committee on the Liturgy, *Eucharistic Concelebration*, Study Text 5, [Washington, D.C.: USCC, 1978], 7).

Signs of Attention and Reverence. According to the *General Instruction* (109) it is permissible to ring a bell as a signal to the people "a little before the consecration" and at each elevation. Yet it is difficult to understand the purpose of such a practice. The people, after all, can see and hear what is taking place. As a sign of reverence, the consecrated bread and wine may be incensed during the elevations (see also *General Instruction*, 235).

Singing. Many presiders (and concelebrating priests) on occasion sing the institution narrative. Yet to preserve the symmetry and unity of the eucharistic prayer this might be more fitting only when other sections of the prayer are also sung, e.g., the preface, concluding doxology, and perhaps the epiclesis. Still, singing individual parts, other than the beginning and conclusion, does tend to fragment the prayer.

Recommended Reading

Bishops' Committee on the Liturgy. "Questions and Answers." *Newsletter* 13, no. 5 (May-June 1977).

Crichton, J. D. *Christian Celebration: The Mass*. London: Geoffrey Chapman, 1971.

Federation of Diocesan Liturgical Commissions. *The Mystery of Faith*. Washington, D.C.: FDLC, 1981.

Memorial Acclamation

A New Element. Immediately after the institution narrative the priest or, as is certainly appropriate, the deacon invites the people to give forth an acclamation "proclaiming the mystery of faith," i.e., the mystery of Christ's death, resurrection, and glorification. It is the total mystery of Christ present and active among his people and still awaited by them. Although such acclamations are not traditionally found in the western church, they occur in several eastern anaphoras where the people sing Amen during the institution narrative. Such formulas do not intrude upon the eucharistic prayer but help support it as a prayer prayed by the priest in the name of all.

Texts. Although only three acclamatory texts appear in the Latin *Order of Mass*, four are found in the Sacramentary, options one and two being different translations of the first Latin formulary. Option one ("Christ has died...") is direct, strong, and perhaps the most popular of all four. Option two ("Dying you destroyed...") is faithful to ancient tradition in that it is addressed to Christ. It is also the most appropriate for use during Advent. The third text ("When we eat this bread...") relates well to occasions when the Eucharist is distributed under both forms. The last option ("Lord, by your cross and resurrection...") is the only formulary that does not mention the second coming.

Since the choice of the text may be made from among a number of options, some communities at times select other formulas for the acclamation. If this is done, the substitution should be acclamatory in nature and not, for example, be a hymn. It should also respect the nature of this acclamation as one proclaiming the "mystery of Christ" in its totality.

Music. Pastoral musicians should take care that the memorial acclamation, being among the most important acclamatory expressions in the liturgy, be sung by the people. Since acclamations are to be spontaneous in nature, lengthy instrumental introductions are to be avoided. Also avoided is the practice of announcing the particular option to be used. When a parish here uses a standard musical repertoire rather than numerous musical settings, the cantor or another minister begins, and all will naturally join in the singing. It is helpful if an instrumentalist gives the deacon or priest a note for his invitation if this also is sung. By so doing, the musician helps the key of the introduction agree with that of the acclamation.

Recommended Reading

Bishops' Committee on the Liturgy. *Music in Catholic Worship*, 57. Washington, D.C.: USCC, 1983.

Deiss, Lucien. *Spirit and Song of the New Liturgy*. Cincinnati: World Library of Sacred Music, 1976.

Federation of Diocesan Liturgical Commissions. *The Mystery of Faith*. Washington, D.C.: FDLC, 1981.

Gelineau, Joseph. *Learning to Celebrate*. Washington, D.C.: The Pastoral Press, 1985.

————. "The Commemorative Acclamation." In *The New Liturgy: A Comprehensive Introduction*. Ed. by Lancelot Sheppard. London: Longman & Todd, 1970.

Anamnesis

General Instruction of the Roman Missal

55e. Anamnesis: in fulfillment of the command received from Christ through the apostles, the Church keeps his memorial by recalling especially his passion, resurrection, and ascension.

A Technical Term. Technically known as the *anamnesis* (from the Greek word for memory and yet expressing a concept that goes far beyond our common understanding of "to remember"), this section recalls that the redeeming actions of Christ are actually made present here and now. The Eucharist is not merely a subjective remembrance of a past event, but an actual, living, and efficacious celebration which contains, as it were, the whole saving action of Christ.

The Texts. The presider proclaims that we, faithful to Christ's command to "Do this in memory of me," indeed make living memorial of his passion (Eucharistic Prayer I), death (II, III, IV), descent among the dead (IV), resurrection (I, II, III, IV), and ascension (I, II, II, IV) as we look forward and are ready to greet him coming again (III, IV).

Recommended Reading

Federation of Diocesan Liturgical Commissions. *The Mystery of Faith*. Washington, D.C.: FDLC, 1981.

Prayer of Offering

General Instruction of the Roman Missal

55f. Offering: in this memorial, the Church — and in particular the Church here and now assembled — offers the spotless victim to the Father in the Holy Spirit. The Church's intention is that the faithful not only offer this victim but also learn to offer themselves and so to surrender themselves, through Christ the Mediator, to an ever more complete union with the Father and with each other, so that at last God may be all in all.

One Sacrifice Offered and Shared. The church, making living memorial of the events of salvation, is thereby enabled to make Christ's offering its very own. For this reason the priest, in the name of all, proclaims that we, i.e., the church, offer a sacrifice which is "holy" (Eucharistic Prayer I, III), "perfect" (I), "living" (III, IV), "acceptable" (IV). We offer the bread "of life" (I), a bread which is "life-giving" (II), as well as a "saving" cup (II), a "cup of salvation" (I). It is also a sacrifice which embraces the lives of all who are united by Christ. The *Constitution on the Liturgy* (48) refers to this offering by the people:

By offering the immaculate Victim, not only through the hands of the priest, but also with him, they should learn to offer themselves as well; through Christ the Mediator, they should be formed day by day into an ever more perfect unity with God and with each other, so that finally God may be all in all.

Recommended Reading

Federation of Diocesan Liturgical Commissions. *The Mystery of Faith*. Washington, D.C.: FDLC, 1981.

Intercessions and Commemorations

General Instruction of the Roman Missal

55g. Intercessions: the intercessions make it clear that the Eucharist is celebrated in communion with the entire Church of heaven and earth and that the offering is made for the Church and all its members, living and dead, who are called to share in the salvation and redemption purchased by Christ's body and blood.

A Community That Remembers and Intercedes. The presence of various petitions in the Jewish meal prayer as well as the church's self-understanding as a community joined to Christ who "forever lives to make intercession" (Heb 7:25) contributed to the early appearance of various intercessory formulas within the eucharistic prayer. The Body of Christ continues to consider it appropriate to pray for its pastors, for the community, for the dead, as well as to invoke the assistance of the saints. Whereas the Roman Canon contains petitions and a listing of the saints both before and after the institution narrative, the recently composed eucharistic prayers locate these before the final doxology. Prayers II and III have special inserts for recalling the names of the deceased. Even though not indicated by the rubrics, it is fitting for the priest to pause at this section of the eucharistic prayer to allow all present to recall privately the names of those persons to be especially remembered.

Recommended Reading

Federation of Diocesan Liturgical Commissions. *The Mystery of Faith*. Washington, D.C.: FDLC, 1981.

Concluding Doxology

General Instruction of the Roman Missal

55h. Final doxology: the praise of God is expressed in the doxology, to which the people's acclamation is an assent and a conclusion.

A Statement of Praise. Just as the eucharistic prayer begins with a strong statement of praise, so it concludes with a laudatory affirmation which is both ancient and solemn. As such it follows the primitive model of the Jewish meal prayer. The presider give glory to the Father through the Son and in the Holy Spirit. This statement is a summation of the Eucharist itself, and thus the people responding "Amen" give their assent or solemnly ratify the whole eucharistic prayer. This Amen was singled out for special mention by St. Justin Martyr writing in the second century: "When the prayer of thanksgiving is ended, everyone present acclaims in a loud voice: 'Amen'. Amen is a Hebrew word meaning: 'So be it'" (*First Apology* 65:3).

The Gesture. The rubrics call for the priest to hold on high the consecrated bread and wine, a gesture of offering accompanying the words of the doxology. When a deacon is present, he stands beside the priest and raises the chalice while the priest raises the plate with the bread. If there is not deacon, a concelebrating priest may elevate the cup. However, only one cup and one breadplate are raised. The visual solemnity of the rite is strengthened if the priest and deacon wait until the conclusion of the people's acclamation before they place the consecrated bread and wine upon the altar.

Singing. Since singing helps bring the eucharistic prayer to a strong and energetic conclusion, presiding priests and concelebrants are encouraged to chant the doxology, even if this can only be done on a straight tone. The instrumentalist might give a soft introductory note so that the key of the priest or priests agrees with that of the people. But even if the "Through him..." cannot be chanted, the people are to sing the final Amen, which is the most important acclamation of the eucharistic celebration. This Amen is to be instantaneous, immediately following upon the statement of praise. A problem, however, is that the two syllables A-men are not strong enough to support an important and dynamic affirmation. Thus, following the tradition of the eastern rites, the Amen is often doubled and even further expanded, at times with embellishments by the choir.

Recommended Reading

Bishops' Committee on the Liturgy. *Music in Catholic Worship*, 58. Washington, D.C.: USCC, 1983.

Crichton, J. D. *Christian Celebration: The Mass*. London: Geoffrey Chapman, 1971.

Deiss, Lucien. *Spirit and Song of the New Liturgy*. Cincinnati: World Library of Sacred Music, 1976.

Federation of Diocesan Liturgical Commissions. *The Mystery of Faith*. Washington, D.C.: FDLC, 1981.

Gelineau, Joseph. *Learning to Celebrate*. Washington, D.C.: The Pastoral Press, 1985.

Walsh, Eugene. *Guidelines for Effective Worship*. Phoenix: North American Liturgy Resources, 1974.

Communion Rite

Overview

General Instruction of the Roman Missal

56. Since the eucharistic celebration is the paschal meal, it is right that the faithful who are properly disposed receive the Lord's body and blood as spiritual food as he commanded. This is the purpose of the breaking of bread and the other preparatory rites that lead directly to the communion of the people.

A Ritual Development. In the earliest celebrations of the Eucharist, the presiding minister, having proclaimed the eucharistic prayer, only had to break the bread and then distribute the consecrated elements to all present. In time, a large number of prayers, chants, and actions were added to provide an elaborate setting for the reception of the Eucharist.

Structure. The *Order of Mass*, while retaining many of these elements, has organized them into a better ordered pattern which embraces three units: a period of preparation, the distribution, and a conclusion. The primary texts would be the Lord's Prayer, the song during the communion procession, and the concluding prayer. The major action preparing for the communion is, of course, the breaking of the bread.

Preparation

Lord's Prayer

Sign of Peace

Breaking of Bread
(accompanied by the Lamb of God)

Commingling

Private preparation of priest and people

Invitation to communion

Distribution

Communion procession and song

Conclusion

Silent prayer/Song of praise

Prayer after communion

Masses with Children. According to the *Directory for Masses with Children* (53) the preparation for communion should always include the Lord's Prayer, the breaking of the bread, and the invitation to communion. There can be adaptations, expansions or omissions of the other rites.

Recommended Reading

Begonja, Tony. *Eucharistic Bread-Baking As Ministry.* San Jose, California: Resource Publications, Inc., 1991.

Bishops' Committee on the Liturgy. *Music in Catholic Worship*, 48. Washington, D.C.: USCC, 1983.

Federation of Diocesan Liturgical Commissions. *The Mystery of Faith.* Washington, D.C.: FDLC, 1981.

Funk, Virgil C., ed., *Music in Catholic Worship: The NPM Commentary.* Washington, D.C.: National Association of Pastoral Musicians, 1982.

Gelineau, Joseph. *Learning to Celebrate.* Washington, D.C.: The Pastoral Press, 1985.

Henchal, Michael. *Sunday Worship in Your Parish.* West Mystic, Connecticut: Twenty-Third Publications, 1980.

Huck, Gabe. *The Communion Rite at Sunday Mass.* Chicago: Liturgy Training Publications, 1989.

Huck, Gabe, ed. *Liturgy with Style and Grace.* Chicago: Liturgy Training Publications, 1984.

Kay, Melissa, ed. *It Is Your Own Mystery.* Washington, D.C.: The Liturgical Conference, 1977.

Keifer, Ralph. *To Give Thanks and Praise.* Washington, D.C.: National Association of Pastoral Musicians, 1980.

Piercy, Robert. "Making Bread for the Eucharist." *Liturgy 90* (February/March 1992).

Lord's Prayer

General Instruction of the Roman Missal

56a. Lord's Prayer: this is a petition both for daily food, which for Christians means also the eucharistic bread, and for the forgiveness of sin, so that what is holy may be given to those who are holy. The priest offers the invitation to pray, but all the faithful say the prayer with him; he alone adds the embolism, *Deliver us,* which the people conclude with a doxology. The embolism, developing the last petition of the Lord's Prayer, begs on behalf of the entire community of the faithful deliverance from the power of evil. The invitation, the prayer itself, the embolism, and the people's doxology are sung or are recited aloud.

110. After the doxology at the end of the eucharistic prayer, the priest, with hands joined, says the introduction to the Lord's Prayer. With hands outstretched he then sings or says this prayer with the people.

111. After the Lord's Prayer, the priest alone, with hands outstretched, says the embolism, *Deliver us.* At the end the congregation makes the acclamation, *For the kingdom.*

Relationship to the Eucharist. The presence of the Lord's Prayer, preparatory to the sharing of Christ's body and blood, has long been traditional in the church, first appearing in the Roman Mass during the fourth century. There are many reasons for its appropriateness, including the following:

1. The prayer requests that we be given "our daily bread," which not only includes the Eucharist but also reminds us of the feasting in God's kingdom, of which the Eucharist is a sign.

2. The prayer asks for the "forgiveness of sins," a petition which several of the church fathers considered to be almost a sacramental occasion of pardon.

3. The prayer reminds us that we are to find peace and unity with our neighbor through forgiving "those who trespass against us."

Structure. The priest introduces the Lord's Prayer by a liturgical invitation (four English versions are given in the Sacramentary) which can and should be adapted to the occasion. All then sing or recite the prayer. Although the bishops of the United States adopted new ecumenical translations for the Gloria and the Creed, they have not done so for the Lord's Prayer. After the prayer the presider alone continues with what is called an embolism, i.e. an interpolated formula extending the last petition of the prayer and requesting perfect peace. Finally, all conclude with the doxology "For the kingdom...," an ancient statement of praise added to the Lord's Prayer to avoid having it end with what has been called a "diabolical finale."

Suggestions for the Presider. It is important that the priest wait till all are standing and attentive before inviting the assembly to pray. Such a pause not only signals that the eucharistic prayer has concluded but also indicates that the assembly is about to begin a new stage in the eucharistic celebration. Since the Lord's Prayer is partially petitionary in content, the extended gesture of the priest might be similar to that used for the opening prayer and others of like content.

Singing. As the primary prayer of preparation for communion, the Lord's Prayer is most fittingly sung. But since it is the prayer of the assembly, it is not sung by the choir alone. Most people readily join in singing the traditional and familiar plainsong melody given in the music section of the Sacramentary. Since the doxology "For the kingdom..." forms a true liturgical conclusion to the Lord's Prayer, this acclamation of praise should be sung whenever the Our Father is sung.

The presence of the embolism can cause musical problems. If the priest is unable to sing the embolism, the integral structure of Lord's Prayer-embolism-doxology can be unified by giving the embolism a very quiet instrumental background leading to a musically forceful doxology. Musical settings of the Lord's Prayer that immediately conclude with the doxology should not be used unless their musical texture can be modified to allow for the priest's embolism.

If much bread is to be broken and is accompanied, as is appropriate, by a lengthy sung Lamb of God, singing both the Our Father and the Lamb of God might add undue weight to what is essentially a preparation rite.

Recommended Reading

Bishops' Committee on the Liturgy. *Music in Catholic Worship*, 59, 67. Washington, D.C.: USCC, 1983.

Emminghaus, Johannes H. *The Eucharist: Essence, Form, Celebration*. Collegeville, Minnesota: The Liturgical Press, 1978.

Federation of Diocesan Liturgical Commissions. *The Mystery of Faith*. Washington, D.C.: FDLC, 1981.

Gelineau, Joseph. *Learning to Celebrate*. Washington, D.C.: The Pastoral Press, 1985.

Smolarski, Dennis. "Q&A: What are the pros and cons of joining hands during the Our Father?" *Liturgy 90* (February/March 1991).

Soubigou, Louis. *A Commentary on the Prefaces and Eucharistic Prayers of the Roman Missal*. Trans. by John A. Otto. Collegeville, Minnesota: The Liturgical Press, 1971.

Walsh, Eugene. *Guidelines for Effective Worship*. Phoenix: North American Liturgy Resources, 1974.

Sign of Peace

General Instruction of the Roman Missal

56b. Rite of peace: before they share in the same bread, the faithful implore peace and unity for the Church and for the whole human family and offer some sign of their love for one another.

The form the sign of peace should take is left to the conference of bishops to determine, in accord with the culture and customs of the people.

112. Then the priest says aloud the prayer, *Lord, Jesus Christ*. After this prayer, extending then joining his hands, he gives the greeting of peace: *The peace of the Lord be with you always*. The people answer: *And also with you*. Then the priest may add: *Let us offer each other a sign of peace*. All exchange some sign of peace and love, according to local custom. The priest may give the sign of peace to the ministers.

History. In the ancient Roman liturgy, the sign of peace, shared at the conclusion of the Liturgy of the Word, was considered as a seal or ratification of what had already taken place. It also looked forward to the presentation of the gifts since the faithful were to be reconciled with each other before bringing gifts to the altar. By the early fourth century, however, its position shifted so that it followed the Our Father, a natural location since the gesture visually expressed the prayer's request that we be forgiven "as we forgive those who sin against us." Whereas for centuries all the faithful exchanged the sign, each with his or her neighbor, the Middle Ages saw the custom arise whereby the priest kissed the altar (representing Christ) and then passed the peace on to the other ministers in proper order. They in turn extended it to the people. In time the people were excluded from the sign. The *Order of Mass* restores this venerable gesture to all the people and, since the peace is rooted in and flows from Christ who is present in the assembly, the handing down of the peace from presider to ministers to people has been happily eliminated.

An Expression of Unity. Peace, resulting from the mutual pardon articulated in the Lord's Prayer, leads to unity. Thus the sign of peace is both a call to as well as a sign of that oneness resulting from membership in the body of Christ. The gesture also gives witness to what it means to be a eucharistic assembly whose members are at peace with one another and who pray and work for the peace of the whole human family. To turn this moment of the celebration into a time for mutual introductions is a misunderstanding of the rite.

Structure. The rite begins with a short prayer, medieval in origin but based upon John 14:27, prayed by the presider with extended hands: "Lord Jesus Christ, you said to your apostles...." This formula is unique since it is the first public prayer (as distinct from an acclamation like the Kyrie) addressed to the Son rather than to the Father. Thereafter the priest, with or perhaps immediately after a gesture of sharing, extends to all the peace of Christ as he says, "The peace of the Lord be with you always." The sincerity and human manner of the minister greatly contribute toward eliciting a vigorous "And also with you" and a true exchange which follows. The deacon or the presider invites all to share the peace. The invitation may be expanded or altered to fit the circumstances of the celebration.

Manner of Celebration. It is left to the conference of bishops to determine the manner in which the peace is to be shared. A 1977 statement of the Bishops' Committee on the Liturgy clarified certain aspects of the practice.

> The manner in which the sign of peace is exchanged
> is to follow the local custom. As a deeply significant
> part of the communion rite, the sign should not be
> used in a casual or introductory way, but should be
> maintained as a true gesture of the mutual peace that
> comes from one's union with Christ. The sign of
> peace may vary according to the type of the
> celebration. In celebrations with large congregations,
> the handshake is the most common. Experience has
> shown that the use of both hands in extending the

greeting creates an expression of greater warmth and distinguishes this rite from the ordinary handclasp associated with a social greeting. Families and close friends might exchange a kiss. In celebrations with smaller groups a handclasp is often used as well as the embrace. Some priests still employ the traditional "pax" of the Roman Rite. Often words accompany the action, such as "Peace be with you" or some similar greeting.

It is also clear that the sign of peace is to be exchanged with persons who are rather close by (*General Instruction* no. 112). Neither the people nor the ministers need try exhaust the sign by attempting to give the greeting personally to everyone in the congregation or even to a great number of those present. The sign remains just that — a sign of the peace that should exist among all those who celebrate the sacrament of unity.

The celebrant of the Eucharist may offer the sign of peace to the deacon or minister, that is, to those near the altar. In accordance with the intent of the ritual, the priest need not move from the altar to offer the sign of peace to other members of the assembly. The reason for this "limited sharing" is that the priest has already prayed for peace among all present and has addressed them with his all inclusive greeting: "The peace of the Lord be with you always."

Unless the sign of peace is clearly tailored to a specific occasion, such as marriage, ordination, or some small intimate group, the more elaborate and individual exchange of peace by the celebrant has a tendency to appear clumsy. It can also accentuate too much the role of the celebrant or ministers, which runs counter to a true understanding of the presence of Christ in the entire assembly. On the other hand, to refrain from offering the sign of peace to some members of the assembly may also on occasion be interpreted by some as a sign of clericalism....

Consideration for the overall ritual flow and rhythm should be an additional important factor in the use of the sign of peace. The time used to

exchange the sign should be in proper proportion to
the other ritual elements of the communion rite and
should not create an imbalance because of the
length, style, musical accompaniment, or other
elements that may give an exaggerated importance to
it. The celebrant, as the one who presides, must
weigh such factors as local standards for propriety,
size of the church, number of participants, character
and intimacy of the assembly, lest the rite become a
mere formality or deteriorate into a frivolous display
(*The Sign of Peace,* USCC, 1977).

Use of Music. At times, e.g., Masses of Reconciliation, the presider may prefer to employ the musical setting of this rite as found
in the Sacramentary. In some communities the exchange of peace
is accompanied by soft instrumental music which leads to the
singing of the Lamb of God. However, the practice of inserting
into the rite a sung text having the theme of peace is generally to
be discouraged since this merely lengthens and overstresses what
is to be a secondary element in a preparatory rite.

Recommended Reading

Bishops' Committee on the Liturgy. "The Sign of Peace." *Newsletter* 7 (January-February 1971).

———. "The Sign of Peace." *Newsletter* 12 (February-March 1976).

———. *The Sign of Peace.* Washington, D.C.: USCC, 1977.

Emminghaus, Johannes H. *The Eucharist: Essence, Form, Celebration.* Collegeville, Minnesota: The Liturgical Press, 1978.

Federation of Diocesan Liturgical Commissions. *The Mystery of Faith.* Washington, D.C.: FDLC, 1981.

Breaking of Bread, Commingling, Lamb of God

General Instruction of the Roman Missal

56c. Breaking of the bread: in apostolic times this
gesture of Christ at the last supper gave the entire
eucharistic action its name. This rite is not simply

functional, but is a sign that in sharing the one bread of life which is Christ we who are many are made one body (see 1 Cor 10:17).

d. Commingling: the celebrant drops a part of the host into the chalice.

e. *Agnus Dei*: during the breaking of the bread and the commingling, the *Agnus Dei* is as a rule sung by the choir or cantor with the congregation responding; otherwise it is recited aloud. This invocation may be repeated as often as necessary to accompany the breaking of the bread. The final reprise concludes with the words, *grant us peace*.

113. The priest then takes the eucharistic bread and breaks it over the paten. He places a small piece in the chalice, saying softly: *May this mingling*. Meanwhile the *Agnus Dei* is sung or recited by the choir and congregation (see no. 56 e).

One Bread, One Body. The breaking of the bread is not only the most primitive rite of preparation for communion but is also a powerful symbol of the assembly's oneness in the eucharistic sharing. Its meaning is explicitly explained by Saint Paul. "The bread that we break, is it not the partaking of the Body of the Lord? Because the bread is one, we though many are one body, all of us who partake of the one bread" (1 Cor 10:16-17). The repetition of this gesture performed by Christ at the Last Supper was considered so important to the early celebration of the Eucharist that the Mass was called "the breaking of the bread."

The Sign Weakens. For many centuries the Roman Church used leavened bread in the celebration of the Eucharist. Originally one large loaf was broken and distributed. As the size of the assembly increased, several loaves were consecrated and broken. For numerous reasons two changes gradually took place: beginning in the ninth century leavened bread was replaced by an unleavened variety; and starting with the tenth century ready-made hosts for the people were introduced. As a result the actual breaking of the bread took place unnoticed and its rich symbolism was simply weakened.

111

Present Desire of the Church. Today the church is calling for the breaking of the bread to reassume its proper importance and meaning. It does so not for reasons of archaeology but for reasons of authenticity. Bread itself is the symbol of life and should therefore look like bread. The breaking of the bread to be shared is an important sign of unity and can take place only if the bread's texture readily allows it to be broken. The *General Instruction* is quite explicit.

> 282. According to the tradition of the entire Church, the bread must be made from wheat; according to the tradition of the Latin Church, it must be unleavened.

> 283. The nature of the sign demands that the material for the eucharistic celebration truly have the appearance of food. Accordingly, even though unleavened and baked in the traditional shape, the eucharistic bread should be made in such a way that in a Mass with a congregation the priest is able actually to break the host into parts and distribute them to at least some of the faithful. (When, however, the number of communicants is large or other pastoral needs require it, small hosts are in no way ruled out.) The action of the breaking of the bread, the simple term for the Eucharist in apostolic times, will more clearly bring out the force and meaning of the sign of the unity of all in the one bread and of their charity, since the one bread is being distributed among the members of one family.

Practical Details. The bread for the Eucharist might be baked by volunteer members of the community. The bread, of course, must be unleavened and, according to present Roman directives, made only from wheat and water. A recipe following such norms is found in *Modern Liturgy* 8:1 (February 1981). Although small hosts are permissible when the assembly is large, the use of a few larger hosts allows the rite to assume a fuller sign value.

The breaking of the bread should not begin until the exchange of peace has been concluded. Deacons (in their absence, communion ministers) assist the presider in this task.

The action should be given prominence: it should not be unduly hurried. Perhaps the bread could be somewhat raised so that all are able to see the action. Since it is not customary to break bread over a drinking glass, the rubrics call for the rite to take place over the paten or breadplate and not the chalice.

To preserve the symbolism of sharing from one bread and one cup, the number of breadplates and chalices should be kept to a minimum. This, however, might seem to pose a problem when the assembly is large.

> A solution is to use one large breadplate and either one large chalice or a large flagon until the breaking of the bread. At the fraction, any other chalices or plates needed are brought to the altar. While the bread is broken on sufficient plates for sharing, the ministers of the cups pour from the flagon into the communion chalices. The number and design of such vessels will depend on the size of the community they serve (*Environment and Art in Catholic Worship*, 96).

Commingling. Throughout its history the Roman Mass incorporated various commingling rites before communion, usually intended to symbolize some aspect of unity. Although the development of these rites is complex and not entirely clear, according to some historians the origin of the present commingling rite may possibly be traced to Syria where an extremely realistic theology of the Eucharist was in vogue. The double consecration, i.e., of bread and then of wine, symbolized Christ's death, i.e., the separation of his body and blood. But since it is the risen Christ who is received in communion, it was judged appropriate also to symbolize the resurrection, i.e., the reuniting of the body and blood. At any rate, the *Order of Mass*, while retaining the action, gives it no special meaning. It is certainly of a very minor importance. The prayer of the priest, "May the mystery...," is a modified version of a text dating from the middle of the eighth century and, as a private formula, is said quietly by the priest.

The Lamb of God. The presence of the Lamb of God dates to the end of the seventh century when Pope Sergius decreed that "during the fraction of the Body of the Lord the Agnus Dei should be sung by the clergy and the people." Thus this chant, originating in the Syrian liturgy, was to accompany an action, i.e., to fill out the interval during which the ministers were breaking the loaves of leavened bread. It was repeated as often as necessary. But with the change from leavened to unleavened bread and with the gradual introduction of small wafer-like hosts for the assembly, the character of this litanic song changed. No longer needed to accompany a lengthy action, it was eventually understood as a preparation for the communion. By the ninth century the formula was said or sung only three times. And beginning with the tenth century, the final termination, "Grant us peace," was added as a reference to the rite of peace, which at that time in Gaul (an ancient region in western Europe) occurred after the breaking of the bread.

Now restored to its original function as accompanying the breaking of the bread, the Lamb of God is sung or said as long as this action continues, another indication that the church desires a real breaking of bread and thus a form of bread whose texture permits this to happen. Although the formula may be recited, it is most appropriately sung, especially when the assembly is large. The intonation may be given by a cantor or by the choir. The musical possibilities are numerous: cantor and assembly; cantor, choir, and assembly; choir and assembly; or assembly alone. The number of repetitions should, of course, be tailored to the length of the action taking place. Should the Lamb of God be recited, the priest or another minister may begin the text, and the priest then immediately proceeds to break the bread while the others continue the litany.

Recommended Reading

Begonja, Tony. *Eucharistic Bread-Baking As Ministry*. San Jose, California: Resource Publications, Inc., 1991.

Bishops' Committee on the Liturgy. *Music in Catholic Worship*, 68. Washington, D.C.: USCC, 1983.

Crichton, J. D. *Christian Celebration: The Mass*. London: Geoffrey Chapman, 1971.

Deiss, Lucien. *Spirit and Song of the New Liturgy*. Cincinnati: World Library of Sacred Music, 1976.

Emminghaus, Johannes H. *The Eucharist: Essence, Form, Celebration*. Collegeville, Minnesota: The Liturgical Press, 1978.

Federation of Diocesan Liturgical Commissions. *The Mystery of Faith*. Washington, D.C.: FDLC, 1981.

Gelineau, Joseph. *Learning to Celebrate*. Washington, D.C.: The Pastoral Press, 1985.

Walsh, Eugene. *Guidelines for Effective Worship*. Phoenix: North American Liturgy Resources, 1974.

Private Preparation of Priest and People

General Instruction of the Roman Missal

56f. Personal preparation of the priest: the priest prepares himself by the prayer, said softly, that he may receive Christ's body and blood to good effect. The faithful do the same by silent prayer.

A Private Prayer. The practice of the priest saying private prayers of preparation before communion dates from the ninth century. Two options for such are given in the *Order of Mass*. As both their wording and the rubrics make clear, this is a private prayer to be said quietly. The assembly, for its part, is to prepare itself not by listening to the words of the presider but by praying in silence. If, for some reason, the Lamb of God is still being sung, the presider should wait till it is concluded before beginning his private preparation. This allows the assembly to have a few similar moments. Instrumentalists should also allow this period of silence to happen.

Concelebration. After the period of preparation and after the presiding priest has genuflected and stepped back, the concelebrants come to the middle of the altar, genuflect, and take the eucharistic bread. They hold the bread in the right hand with the left under it, and then return to their places. Another procedure is for the concelebrants to remain in their places and take the consecrated bread from a communion plate passed from one to another or held by the presiding priest, by the deacon, or by one of the concelebrating priests.

Invitation to Communion

General Instruction of the Roman Missal

115. After the prayer the priest genuflects, takes the eucharistic bread, and, holding it slightly above the paten while facing the people, says: *This is the Lamb of God*. With the people he adds, once only: *Lord, I am not worthy to receive you*.

"Holy Things to the Holy." This is the popular form of invitation to communion found in the eastern churches. The Roman Church, however, uses a combination of New Testament texts (see Jn 1:29; Rv 19:9; Mt 8:9) to express the same meaning. The presider's invitation may be adapted to the feast or occasion. And when there is concelebration, only the presiding priest shows the eucharistic bread to the assembly.

Recommended Reading

Emminghaus, Johannes H. *The Eucharist: Essence, Form, Celebration*. Collegeville, Minnesota: The Liturgical Press, 1978.

Federation of Diocesan Liturgical Commissions. *The Mystery of Faith*. Washington, D.C.: FDLC, 1981.

Distribution of the Eucharist

General Instruction of the Roman Missal

116. Next, facing the altar, the priest says softly: *May the body of Christ bring me to everlasting life* and reverently consumes the body of Christ. Then he takes the chalice, saying: *May the blood of Christ bring*

me to everlasting life, and reverently drinks the blood of Christ.

117. He then takes the paten or a ciborium and goes to the communicants. If communion is given only under the form of bread, he raises the eucharistic bread slightly and shows it to each one, saying: *The body of Christ.* The communicants reply: *Amen* and, holding the communion plate under their chin, receive the sacrament.

Hierarchical Structure. Although some argue that the presiding minister, like the host of a meal, should be the last to receive the body and blood of the Lord, the distribution of the Eucharist in all rites follows a hierarchical structure with the presider being the first to communicate.

Private Texts. Being stimulants for the private devotion of the priest, the texts "May the body..." and "May the blood..." are said inaudibly. The Latin is *secreto.*

Concelebration. Concelebrants quietly say "May the body..." with the principal concelebrant and then consume the eucharistic bread. Although the consecrated wine may be received through a tube, with a spoon, or by intinction, receiving directly from the cup is the almost universal practice. There are several ways of doing this, including:

- The presiding celebrant, after drinking from the cup, hands it to a deacon or concelebrant. The concelebrants approach the altar one by one or in pairs if two cups are used. They receive from the cup and then return to their places. A deacon or concelebrant wipes the chalice with a purificator after each priest receives.

- The concelebrants remain in their places while the principal concelebrant receives from the cup. Then the deacon or one of the concelebrants takes the cup and presents it to the concelebrants. It may also be handed from one to another. The chalice should always be wiped, either by the one who drinks from it or by the person presenting it.

- It is also possible for the concelebrants to receive from the chalice at the altar immediately after they receive the body of Christ. In this case the presiding priest communicates under both kinds, and the chalice is placed on another corporal at the right side of the altar. Each concelebrant comes forward, genuflects, and receives the eucharistic bread. He then goes to the side of the altar and drinks the consecrated wine.

Special Ministers of the Eucharist. Since the 1973 publication of the instruction *Immensae Caritatis* many dioceses designate qualified non-ordained men and women to serve the assembly as special ministers of the Eucharist. The purpose of this ministry is to compensate for the lack of sufficient ordinary ministers of communion when there are many communicants. When special ministers are lacking, the distribution of the Eucharist is so prolonged that it unbalances the structural equilibrium of the whole celebration. Moreover, a minimal homily is often preached, periods of silence are omitted, and the shortest eucharistic prayer is used. Furthermore, although there may be an adequate number of priests in some parishes, one may question the appropriateness of ordained ministers suddenly appearing from the sacristy, distributing communion, and then immediately disappearing from the assembly.

Individual dioceses and parishes have particular norms regarding the manner in which special ministers function. The Bishops' Committee on the Liturgy, however, has specified that the following procedures be observed.

1. During the breaking of the bread and the commingling, the ministers go to and stand near the altar. They may also assist by pouring the consecrated wine from the flagons into communion cups.

2. After the presiding priest (and concelebrants) have received communion, the ministers receive from the priest.

3. Special ministers are encouraged to receive under both kinds. The deacon or priest offers them the cup.

4. Then the priest give the ministers the ciborium or other vessel with the eucharistic bread. They may also act as ministers of the cup.

5. Then the ministers distribute to the faithful.

These ministers may also bring the Eucharist to the sick and other shut-ins. Through such a ministry the infirm and aged are able to partake of communion as well as to be linked with the community at worship, the gathering in which they physically participated for so many years. In some communities, immediately before the final blessing, the ministers are presented with pyxes containing the eucharistic bread which they, often accompanied by family members, bring to those unable to be present as members of the assembly.

Recommended Reading

Bishops' Committee on the Liturgy. "Extraordinary Ministers of Communion." *Newsletter* 12, no. 6 (August, 1976).

———. *Holy Communion: Commentary on the Instruction Immensae Caritatis.* Study Text 1. Washington, D.C.: USCC, 1973.

———. "Instruction on the Eucharist." *Newsletter* 9, no. 3 (February 1973).

Huck, Gabe. *The Communion Rite at Sunday Mass.* Chicago: Liturgy Training Publications, 1989.

Sharing in the Sacrifice Being Celebrated. As already mentioned, the people are to receive the Eucharist from one bread broken into parts after the exchange of peace. Yet, when the number of communicants is large, small hosts may be used. These, too, are to be consecrated during the same Mass at which they are received. This was the centuries old tradition of the church, one even presumed in the Missal of Pius V. Starting from the eighteenth century, however, the pretext of convenience was used to justify the practice of using hosts consecrated at a previous Mass and reserved in the tabernacle.

Such a procedure, however, greatly weakens the unity of the rite in which there is a close link between the consecration and the reception of the bread and wine. As early as 1967, the *Instruction on Worship of the Eucharist* (31) stated:

> In order that the communion may stand out more
> clearly even through signs as a participation in the
> sacrifice actually being celebrated, steps should be
> taken that enable the faithful to receive hosts
> consecrated at that Mass.

Consequently, the minister should use pieces of the large host or hosts broken at the fraction and, when necessary, other hosts consecrated at the same celebration. Routinely retrieving hosts from the tabernacle for the sake of convenience is contrary not only to good liturgical practice but also to the explicit desire of the church.

"Take and Drink." For centuries Christians received both the consecrated bread and the consecrated wine. But by the end of the thirteenth century, a change in liturgical practice occurred. Fear of spilling the contents of the cup, fear of contracting disease, the development of the doctrine that the whole Christ is received even under one form, all contributed to the loss of the lay chalice. Nevertheless, reception under both kinds continued to remain the normal practice in the East.

Today, the Roman Church, while respecting an individual's freedom of choice, encourages communion under both kinds. According to the *General Instruction* (240):

> Holy communion has a more complete form as a sign
> when it is received under both kinds. For in this
> manner of reception a fuller light shines on the sign
> of the eucharistic banquet. Moreover there is a
> clearer expression of that will by which the new and
> everlasting covenant is ratified in the blood of the
> Lord and of the relationship of the eucharistic
> banquet to the eschatological banquet in the Father's
> kingdom.

The reason for receiving both the eucharistic bread and wine, therefore, is not to be found in the theological reality but rather in the sign value of the sacrament. At the Last Supper the command of Jesus was not only "Take and eat" but also "Take and drink." The Mass, being both sacrifice and meal, has a fuller sign value when the assembly not only partakes of the eucharistic bread but also shares in the eucharistic cup. Furthermore, the cup is the sign of the new covenant (see Lk 22:20), the guarantee and expectation of the heavenly banquet (see Mk 26:29), and the sign of union with the Christ who suffered (see Mk 10:38-39).

Recent years have witnessed a gradual extension of occasions when, with the approval of the bishop, communion from the cup is allowed. The *General Instruction* (242) lists fourteen occasions when this is permitted. In 1970 the bishops of the United States added another five occasions, including all weekday Masses. And in 1978 the bishops voted to extend permission to the Sunday assembly. Thus, presuming the permission of the bishop, there is no occasion when the Eucharist may not be distributed under both forms.

The most common and certainly the preferred method of receiving the eucharistic wine is by sharing from a communion cup or chalice. Here the sign value of the action is apparent since what is important is not the material consumption of the wine but the expression of the complete sign, namely eating and drinking. Distributing from the cup may pose logistic problems in large assemblies, and yet solutions are usually found through the use of well prepared special ministers. Correctly determining the amount of wine to be consecrated may also pose an initial problem. Experience will provide an answer.

In no case should the cup be placed upon the altar or on a table from which the communicants help themselves. This simply depersonalizes the sacrament, and sacraments always are to involve people interacting with other people. Following the ancient tradition of the church, there should always be a minister who presents the cup. Minister and communicant form in miniature what the community is all about, i.e., people serving other people and being served by other people.

It is also possible to distribute the wine by the use of a metal straw, with a spoon, or by intinction. While the first two of these options are rare, some communities at times use intinction, i.e., dipping the eucharistic bread into the consecrated wine as is customary in the churches of the East. Only the minister may intinct the eucharistic bread in the consecrated wine; the communicant may not dip the bread him- or herself (see Bishops' Committee on the Liturgy, *This Holy and Living Sacrifice*, 52). This option is far from ideal since it precludes the action of drinking. However, should intinction be employed, the bread's texture must be able to absorb the wine. Furthermore, communion is not to be distributed in the hand when intinction is used. Nor should intinction be a means of circumventing communion in the hand.

Recommended Reading

Belgian Interdiocesan Liturgical Commission. "The Liturgical and Spiritual Importance of Communion from the Chalice." In Bishops' Committee on the Liturgy, *Newsletter* 14, no. 8 (October 1978).

Bishops' Committee on the Liturgy. "Communion under Both Kinds." *Newsletter* 2, no. 7 (July 1966).

———. "Communion under Both Kinds." *Newsletter* 7, (January-February 1971).

———. "Communion under Both Kinds." *Newsletter* 15, no. 1 (January 1979).

———. "Communion under Both Kinds on Sunday." *Newsletter* 10, no. 10 (October 1974).

————. "The Distribution of Communion." *Newsletter* 10, no. 11 (November 1974).

————. *This Holy and Living Sacrifice: Directory for the Celebration and Reception of Communion under Both Kinds.* Washington, D.C.: USCC, 1985.

Crichton, J. D. *Christian Celebration: The Mass.* London: Geoffrey Chapman, 1971.

Emminghaus, Johannes H. *The Eucharist: Essence, Form, Celebration.* Collegeville, Minnesota: The Liturgical Press, 1978.

Huck, Gabe. *The Communion Rite at Sunday Mass.* Chicago: Liturgy Training Publications, 1989.

Communion Procession. It is for each community to develop a well-ordered procession of communicants. The use of several locations or stations at which the people receive facilitates the distribution. And yet, if possible, all such stations should be located toward the front of the church so as to preserve the character of a procession whose participants — as members of one body — together approach the table of the Lord. Ushers may be of great assistance in facilitating the movement of the assembly, and yet they should do so in a reverent and unobtrusive manner. Many consider as far from ideal the practice whereby ushers signal the communicants to leave their places and enter the procession since this can easily infringe upon a person's complete freedom to communicate or to refrain from so doing.

Standing or Kneeling. Two postures, i.e., standing or kneeling, are possible while receiving communion. The more ancient is that of standing which recalls that those who communicate are a people risen with the Lord through baptism. In fact, the Council of Nicaea in 325 explicitly prohibited Christians from kneeling on Sunday, the day of the Lord's resurrection. Even from a practical aspect, standing facilitates an orderly and quick procession. Kneeling, a posture expressing adoration, dates from the Middle Ages and was never prescribed by the rubrics.

According to the 1967 *Instruction on Worship of the Eucharist*, national episcopal conferences may choose either of the two postures. Although the bishops of the United States have not done so, standing has received almost universal acceptance in our country. The same document (34a) also states that "the faithful should willingly follow the manner of reception indicated by the pastors so that communion may truly be a sign of familial union among all those who share in the same table of the Lord."

The Profession of Faith. The minister of the Eucharist is to hold the eucharistic bread before each communicant, raise it a little, and show it while saying, "The Body of Christ." The communicant responds, "Amen," and receives the bread of life from the ministers. When distributing from the cup, the minister says, "The Blood of Christ," and the communicant responds "Amen." Then the minister holds out the cup and purificator. The communicant raises the cup to his or her mouth and then, holding the purificator under the mouth with the left hand, drinks a little of the precious blood. The minister, upon receiving back the cup, wipes it with the purificator. In practice, however, most ministers retain the purificator which they use to wipe the rim of the cup, both inside and out.

Formulas accompanying the distribution of communion are traditional in both East and West. St. Augustine (354-430) explains the meaning of the phrase, "The Body of Christ."

> What is meant by one bread? St. Paul interpreted it
> briefly: "We being many, are one body." This bread is
> the body of Christ, to which the Apostle refers when
> he addressed the Church: "Now you are the body of
> Christ and his members." That which you receive,
> that you yourselves are by the grace of the
> redemption, as you acknowledge when you respond
> Amen. What you witness here is the sacrament of
> unity (*Sermon* 272).

The Amen, then, is not a "Thank you" but a profession of faith in three realities: the presence of Christ in the assembly, the presence of Christ in the communicant, and the presence of Christ under the forms of bread and wine. For the minister to say, "This is the Body..." or "Receive the Body...," simply restricts the meaning of the phrase and weakens its rich unitive significance.

Ministers should avoid all haste and routine in the rite of distribution. This is to be a human, faith-filled experience. By the tone of voice, by human expression and warmth, by looking at the communicant, the minister is to evoke a heartfelt and sincere response of belief in Christ's multi-dimensional and ever-deepening presence among his people.

Recommended Reading

Bishops' Committee on the Liturgy. "The Body of Christ." *Newsletter* 12, no. 9 (September 1976).

Huck, Gabe. *The Communion Rite at Sunday Mass.* Chicago: Liturgy Training Publications, 1989.

Communion in the Hand. For centuries people received the eucharistic bread in their hands. A classic description of this manner of communicating is given by St. Cyril of Jerusalem (315-386).

> When you approach, do not come forward holding
> the palms of your hands extended, and your fingers
> separated. But, since your right hand will bear the
> King, make for him a throne with your left hand, and
> in the hollow of your hand receive the Body of Christ
> and respond: Amen (Mystagogical Catechesis V. 21).

With the introduction of small, wafer-like hosts into the western church and with the development of an exaggerated feeling of unworthiness, the laity began to receive the bread on the tongue. By the ninth century, communion in the hand was no longer the universal practice.

The years after Vatican II saw a growing desire to allow people the option of receiving the eucharistic bread in the hand. Since 1969 episcopal conferences have been allowed to ask Rome for permission to introduce or to continue (where the practice previously arose) communion in the hand as an option, provided careful instruction be given. In the spring of 1977 the United States bishops voted to request this permission which was granted on June 17 of the same year.

The principal reason for such a return to tradition is that communion in the hand calls for a more natural and less infantile attitude on the part of the communicant. It is also expressive of a more active and human response to the invitation, "Take and eat." Moreover, such a method is certainly more sanitary than communion distributed on the tongue.

When receiving communion in the hand the communicant approaches the priest or other minister of communion with hands uncovered. One hand rests upon the other, palm up, ordinarily the left hand uppermost. He or she extends the hands in a reverent manner so that the bread may be placed easily upon the open but hollowed palm. The bread of life is held momentarily before the communicant as the minister addresses the person with the words, "The Body of Christ." After the communicant responds, "Amen," the minister places the host in the hand. If necessary, the person steps to one side and gives place to the next communicant and immediately, taking the host in the right hand, consumes the eucharistic bread. Only then does the communicant return to his or her place.

Recommended Reading

Bishops' Committee on the Liturgy. "Holy See Approves Communion in the Hand." *Newsletter* 13, no. 8 (August 1977).

Emminghaus, Johannes H. *The Eucharist: Essence, Form, Celebration.* Collegeville, Minnesota: The Liturgical Press, 1978.

Communion Song

General Instruction of the Roman Missal

56i. During the priest's and the faithful's reception of the sacrament the communion song is sung. Its function is to express outwardly the communicants' union in spirit by means of the unity of their voices, to give evidence of joy of heart, and to make the procession to receive Christ's body more fully an act of the community. The song begins when the priest takes communion and continues for as long as seems appropriate while the faithful receive Christ's body.

But the communion song should be ended in good
time whenever there is to be a hymn after
communion.

An antiphon from the *Graduale Romanum* may
also be used, with or without the psalm, or an
antiphon with psalm from *The Simple Gradual* or
another suitable song approved by the conference of
bishops. It is sung by the choir alone or by the choir
of cantor with the congregation.

If there is no singing, the communion antiphon in
the Missal is recited by the people, by some of them,
or by a reader. Otherwise the priest himself says it
after he has received communion and before he gives
communion to the faithful.

Oneness in Christ. Just as song accompanies the initial procession of the ministers and the procession of those presenting the
gifts, so too does song accompany the procession of the communicants. In this case it is a sign of joy, an act manifesting that unity
shared by those who partake of the one body and blood of the
Lord. Although the reception of communion is a personal action,
it is also a public action of the community worshiping together.

Choice of Texts. The tradition of the Roman rite has been to link
the plainsong text of the entrance song (Introit) to the liturgical
season or feast and to give the communion song a more general
character. Texts expressive of unity, encounter with the Lord, joy,
etc., are always appropriate. The majority of texts used at Bene-
diction are not suitable at this time since they emphasize adoration rather than communion. During the important cycles of the
liturgical year the texts might also be seasonal in nature.

Choice of Music. Experience shows that participation is more
readily elicited by using responsorial texts rather than metrical
hymns. A short repeated refrain is easily memorized, eliminating
the need for people to hold hymnals or songsheets in the procession. Such worship aids are especially cumbersome when communicants use their legitimate option of receiving communion in
the hand.

127

On occasion a choir selection might be fitting during the procession. In this case a song of praise is most appropriate after the communion.

When to Begin. The song is to accompany the assembly's reception of communion. The ministers are part of this assembly. Thus the *General Instruction*, to avoid fragmenting what is essentially one rite, states that the communion song begins as the priest receives the eucharistic bread and wine. It continues "for as long as seems appropriate." The cantor and instrumentalists, therefore, would be the last to receive.

Some Options. When the assembly is large, it might be advantageous to allow some "breathing space" within the singing. This can be accomplished by a short instrumental interlude after every two or three verses. Another possibility is to proclaim a short scriptural text after the verses. When these can be selected from the readings used in the Liturgy of the Word, the practice serves to link the two parts of the celebration.

Recommended Reading

Bishops' Committee on the Liturgy. *Music in Catholic Worship*, 62. Washington, D.C.: USCC, 1983.

Crichton, J. D. *Christian Celebration: The Mass*. London: Geoffrey Chapman, 1971.

Deiss, Lucien. *Spirit and Song of the New Liturgy*. Cincinnati: World Library of Sacred Music, 1976.

Emminghaus, Johannes H. *The Eucharist: Essence, Form, Celebration*. Collegeville, Minnesota: The Liturgical Press, 1978.

Federation of Diocesan Liturgical Commissions. *The Mystery of Faith*. Washington, D.C.: FDLC, 1981.

Gelineau, Joseph. *Learning to Celebrate*. Washington, D.C.: The Pastoral Press, 1985.

Huck, Gabe. *The Communion Rite at Sunday Mass*. Chicago: Liturgy Training Publications, 1989.

Walsh, Eugene. *Guidelines for Effective Worship*. Phoenix: North American Liturgy Resources, 1974.

Cleansing of the Vessels

General Instruction of the Roman Missal

120. After communion the priest returns to the altar and collects any remaining particles. Then, standing at the side of the altar or at a side table, he purifies the paten or ciborium over the chalice, then purifies the chalice, saying quietly: *Lord, may I receive these gifts*, etc., and dries it with a purificator. If this is done at the altar, the vessels are taken to a side table by a minister. It is also permitted, especially if there are several vessels to be purified, to leave them, properly covered and on a corporal, either at the altar or at a side table and to purify them after Mass when the people have left.

238. The vessels are purified by the priest or else by the deacon or acolyte after the communion or after Mass, if possible at a side table. Wine and water or water alone are used for the purification of the chalice, then drunk by the one who purifies it. The paten is usually to be wiped with the purificator.

By Whom. Either the presiding priest, the deacon, an instituted acolyte, or a special communion minister may purify the vessels. Being functional in nature, the task should be accomplished as discreetly and as expeditiously as reverence and decorum allow.

Where. If the presider purifies the vessels, he does so at the side (not the middle) of the altar or, preferably, at a side table. The deacon, acolyte, and special minister do so at the table.

When. The cleansing of the vessels may occur either immediately after the distribution or after the close of the celebration. Many prefer the latter option since it allows the ministers more time for prayer and reflection.

The Prayer. The text is prayed by the priest in an inaudible manner.

Recommended Reading

Bishops' Committee on the Liturgy. "The Purification of the Vessels." *Newsletter* 15 (May 1979).

Emminghaus, Johannes H. *The Eucharist: Essence, Form, Celebration.* Collegeville, Minnesota: The Liturgical Press, 1978.

Federation of Diocesan Liturgical Commissions. *The Mystery of Faith.* Washington, D.C.: FDLC, 1981.

Silent Prayer/Song of Praise

General Instruction of the Roman Missal

56j. After communion, the priest and people may
spend some time in silent prayer. If desired, a hymn,
psalm, or other song of praise may be sung by the
entire congregation.

Silent Prayer. After the communion the assembly may spend some moments in silent prayer. Such a period offers each member of the community an opportunity for meditation, for reflection on the transforming power of Christ in his members, especially as they continue the work of Christ by transforming the world in which they live. This interval may, at times, be judiciously supported yet never supplanted by visual aids, brief meditative readings, and other means that help elicit true prayer. The prayer after communion thus sums up the silent prayers of all.

Song of Praise. Another option is for the assembly to sing a hymn, psalm, or other song of praise. It is with purpose that the *General Instruction* speaks of a "song of praise" since the motif here is different from that of the communion song which ordinarily expresses unity and communion. If the whole assembly sings a refrain during the communion procession, a hymn at this point rather than responsorial singing offers some contrast. At any rate, common song here is certainly most appropriate on those occasions when the choir alone sings during the communion procession. The appropriate posture for this song is standing.

Communion Litany. Some communities substitute a litany of praise or thanksgiving for the song after the communion. After a short period of silent prayer the presider invites all to pray. Then a reader recites or a cantor sings various invocations to which all respond. These invocations are not petitionary as those found in the general intercessions. Rather, they might be based on the scripture readings for the day or simply state general motives for praise, e.g., "For the gift of your living presence among us...." The invocation might conclude with a standard cue phrase, e.g., "Let us praise the Lord." The people's response might be, "We indeed praise you, O Lord," or something similar. At the litany's conclusion the priest immediately begins the prayer after communion.

Recommended Reading

Bishops' Committee on the Liturgy. *Music in Catholic Worship*, 72. Washington, D.C.: USCC, 1983.

Deiss, Lucien. *Spirit and Song of the New Liturgy*. Cincinnati: World Library of Sacred Music, 1976.

Emminghaus, Johannes H. *The Eucharist: Essence, Form, Celebration*. Collegeville, Minnesota: The Liturgical Press, 1978.

Federation of Diocesan Liturgical Commissions. *The Mystery of Faith*. Washington, D.C.: FDLC, 1981.

Gelineau, Joseph. *Learning to Celebrate*. Washington D.C.: The Pastoral Press, 1985

Prayer after Communion

General Instruction of the Roman Missal

56k. In the prayer after communion, the priest petitions for the effects of the mystery just celebrated and by their acclamation, *Amen*, the people make the prayer their own.

122. Then, standing at the altar or at the chair and facing the people, the priest says, with hands outstretched: *Let us pray*. There may be a brief period

of silence, unless this has already been observed
immediately after communion. He recites the prayer
after communion, at the end of which the people
make the response: *Amen.*

Content. This prayer, concluding the communion rite, recalls the gifts of the Eucharist and requests that it might bear fruit in our lives. Unlike the opening prayer, it is rarely connected with a feast or season. Nor is it expressive of thanksgiving, this being the motif of the eucharistic prayer, especially the preface.

Some Practicalities. Announcements are not to be given before this prayer since this simply fractures the integrity and rhythm of the communion rite. Nor should the people be verbally requested to stand: the action of the presider rising is a sufficient signal for all to do likewise. Although the *General Instruction* mentions that the priest may say the prayer either at the altar (presumably because the prayer concludes the communion rite) or at the presider's chair, it is more common for him to do so at the chair where he has participated in silent prayer or sung praise with the other members of the assembly. The *General Instruction* also reminds the presider that when silence has occurred after the distribution, it is superfluous to repeat this silence after the "Let us pray." And, as with the prayer over the gifts, the presider terminates the formula with the short conclusion.

Recommended Reading

Emminghaus, Johannes H. *The Eucharist: Essence, Form, Celebration*. Collegeville, Minnesota: The Liturgical Press, 1978.

Federation of Diocesan Liturgical Commissions. *The Mystery of Faith*. Washington, D.C.: FDLC, 1981.

4.

CONCLUDING RITES

Overview

Leave-Taking. Saying farewell until we meet again is a part, be it formal or informal, of most human gatherings. It often implies a togetherness in spirit and purpose as those who share in a common event disperse to pursue other endeavors. It was only natural, then, for the Mass to develop a formal conclusion, usually consisting of a blessing over the assembly, or a dismissal of the assembly, or both. Although always remaining brief, these rites had a tendency to expand in number and vary in sequence.

Structure. Today the concluding rites consist of:

Announcements

Blessing

Dismissal

Recession of the ministers

The blessing is the most important element. On occasions when another liturgical service follows the Mass, all the concluding rites are simply omitted.

Recommended Reading

Federation of Diocesan Liturgical Commissions. *The Mystery of Faith*. Washington, D.C.: FDLC, 1981.

Huck, Gabe, ed. *Liturgy with Style and Grace*. Chicago: Liturgy Training Publications, 1984.

Announcements

General Instruction of the Roman Missal

123. If there are any brief announcements, they may be made at this time.

Only When Necessary and Always Brief. Only those notifications which are absolutely necessary should be given. They should always be brief, especially when they already appear in a printed bulletin. This might also be a suitable time for reading letters and other communications from the bishop.

By Whom. Some communities deem it more appropriate that announcements regarding bingo, PTA meetings, etc., be given by a minister other than the presider. And yet if done by the priest, the most appropriate place would be from the presidential chair, certainly not from the ambo.

Recommended Reading

Emminghaus, Johannes H. *The Eucharist: Essence, Form, Celebration.* Collegeville, Minnesota: The Liturgical Press, 1978.

Federation of Diocesan Liturgical Commissions. *The Mystery of Faith.* Washington, D.C.: FDLC, 1981.

Blessing

General Instruction of the Roman Missal

57. The concluding rite consists of:
a. the priest's greeting and blessing, which on certain days and occasions is expanded and expressed in the prayer over the people or another more solemn formulary;....

124. Then the priest, with hands outstretched, greets the people: *The Lord be with you.* They answer: *And also with you.* The priest immediately adds: *May almighty God bless you* and, as he blesses with the sign of the cross, continues: *the Father, and the Son, and the Holy Spirit.* All answer: *Amen.* On certain days and occasions another more solemn form of blessing or the prayer over the people precedes this form of blessing as the rubrics direct.

Greeting. The traditional "The Lord be with you" with its response serves as a formal introduction to the blessing.

Blessing. This may be given in its simple form, i.e., "May almighty God bless you...." The presider may also employ one of two expanded forms, i.e., the solemn blessing or the prayer over the people.

When either of the two expansions is used, the deacon or, in his absence, the presider, gives the invitation, "Bow your heads...." Other invitatory formulas, always short and similar in content, may be improvised.

The Sacramentary provides a solemn blessing for Advent, Christmas, the Beginning of the New Year, Epiphany, the Passion of the Lord, the Easter Vigil and Easter Sunday, the Easter Season, Ascension, Holy Spirit, Ordinary Time (five versions), the Blessed Virgin, Peter and Paul, the Apostles, All Saints, the Dedication of a Church, and the Dead. These ordinarily have a tripartite structure, each section concluding with the people responding Amen. This response is greatly facilitated by the presider singing the blessing. The Sacramentary contains two possible musical formulas. Even when the priest can only sing the formula on a straight tone with a drop of the voice at the end of each clause, the assembly knows precisely when to answer. When the blessing is not sung, it is the tone, stress, and the eye contact of the priest which must indicate the moment for the response.

The prayer of the people consists of an oration prayed by the presider over all assembled. Such prayers were once used frequently in the liturgy, but their occurrence was gradually restricted to the weekdays of Lent. Now restored, some twenty-six formulas for the prayer are included in the Sacramentary.

In both options the priest is to extend his hand out and over the people as a sign of asking God's power and strength to descend upon them. The extension of only one hand lacks completeness and visual balance. Thus the book, as when always used at the presidential chair, is held by a deacon or other minister.

Whatever be the form of the blessing, the presider always calls upon the Trinity as he makes the sign of the cross. Just as the Trinity was formally invoked during the introductory rites, so all are now blessed in the name of the same Divine Persons.

Recommended Reading

Emminghaus, Johannes H. *The Eucharist: Essence, Form, Celebration.* Collegeville, Minnesota: The Liturgical Press, 1978.

Federation of Diocesan Liturgical Commissions. *The Mystery of Faith.* Washington, D.C.: FDLC, 1981.

Krosnicki, Thomas A. "New Blessings in the Missal of Paul VI." *Worship* 45, no. 4 (April 1971): 199-205.

International Committee on English in the Liturgy. *Book of Blessings.* Collegeville, Minnesota: The Liturgical Press, 1989.

Dismissal

General Instruction of the Roman Missal

57b. ...the dismissal of the assembly which sends each member back to doing good works, while praising and blessing the Lord.

124. Immediately after the blessing, with hands joined, the priest adds: *Go in the peace of Christ,* or *Go in peace to love and serve the Lord,* or: *The Mass is ended, go in peace,* and the people answer: *Thanks be to God.*

Go in Peace. The deacon or, in his absence, the priest dismisses the assembly by using one of the formulas found in the Sacramentary. These texts, however, may be adapted to the occasion.

The traditional Roman dismissal text *Ite, missa est,* literally, "Go, it is over," is a liturgical borrowing of a dismissal formula used at Roman secular gatherings. The three translations of this Latin text in the Sacramentary are all scripturally inspired (see, e.g., Mk 5:34) as is often the custom for the dismissal in various eastern liturgies. The assembly is bidden to depart in the peace of Christ as its members prepare to go forth and live what they have just celebrated.

Recommended Reading

Emminghaus, Johannes H. *The Eucharist: Essence, Form, Celebration*. Collegeville, Minnesota: The Liturgical Press, 1978.

Federation of Diocesan Liturgical Commissions. *The Mystery of Faith*. Washington, D.C.: 1981.

Recession of the Ministers

General Instruction of the Roman Missal

125. As a rule, the priest then kisses the altar, makes the proper reverence with the ministers, and leaves.

Procession. Only the presider and the deacon kiss the altar as a farewell gesture of respect. Then all the ministers, including any concelebrants, either bow profoundly toward the altar or, if the tabernacle with the reserved sacrament is in the sanctuary, genuflect toward it.

The *General Instruction* gives no details regarding the exit procession of the ministers. Its pace is usually more rapid than that of the entrance procession. It has also become customary for the exit to mirror the entrance procession with the reader carrying the Book of the Gospels or Lectionary, a server carrying the cross, etc. At any rate, the procession here is a functional action and is to be carried out as such.

Recessional Song. Although not an integral part of the liturgy, the use of a sung recessional is common in most communities. Yet music planners need determine what they desire to happen here and choose among the various options available to them.

If the choice is to allow the assembly to participate actively in a concluding statement of faith and joy, then a hymn sung by all may be appropriate. Its text can relate to the particular occasion or may be of a general nature. If the thematic development of the hymn allows, concluding verses of the entrance song may at times be fitting. The piece should always be strong in character and familiar. It is a good sign for all the ministers to delay their exit till toward the conclusion of the singing. This also encourages all to remain and join in the common song. And yet, it must be remembered that singing during the communion procession, after the distribution of communion, and again at the end of the celebration musically overpowers the structural equilibrium of the celebration.

If the desire is to provide a joyful concluding atmosphere for the departure of ministers and people, then instrumental music or a choir selection may be preferred.

During certain seasons of the year, the choice may be to allow all to depart in silence.

Recommended Reading

Bishops' Committee on the Liturgy. *Music in Catholic Worship*, 73. Washington, D.C.: USCC, 1983.

Deiss, Lucien. *Spirit and Song of the New Liturgy*. Cincinnati: World Library of Sacred Music, 1976.

Federation of Diocesan Liturgical Commissions. *The Mystery of Faith*. Washington, D.C.: FDLC, 1981.

Gelineau, Joseph. *Learning to Celebrate*. Washington, D.C.: The Pastoral Press, 1985.

Walsh, Eugene. *Guidelines for Effective Worship*. Phoenix: North American Liturgy Resources, 1974.

Select Bibliography

Books Often Cited in the Text

Bishops' Committee on the Liturgy. *Music in Catholic Worship*. Rev. ed. Washington, D.C.: USCC, 1983.

Crichton, J. D. *Christian Celebration: The Mass*. London: Geoffrey Chapman, 1971.

Deiss, Lucien. *Spirit and Song of the New Liturgy*. Rev. ed. Trans. by Lyla L. Haggard and Michael L. Mazzarese. Cincinnati: World Library of Sacred Music, 1976.

Emminghaus, Johannes H. *The Eucharist: Essence, Form, Celebration*. Trans. by Matthew J. O'Connell. Collegeville, Minnesota: The Liturgical Press, 1978.

Federation of Diocesan Liturgical Commissions. *The Mystery of Faith: A Study of the Structural Elements of the Mass*. Washington, D.C.: FDLC, 1981.

Funk, Virgil C., ed. *Music in Catholic Worship: The NPM Commentary: A Collection of Articles First Published in Pastoral Music Magazine*. Washington, D.C.: National Association of Pastoral Musicians, 1982.

Gelineau, Joseph. *Learning to Celebrate: The Mass and Its Music*. Washington, D.C.: The Pastoral Press, 1985.

Henchal, Michael J. *Sunday Worship in Your Parish: What It Is, What It Could Be*. West Mystic, Connecticut: Twenty-Third Publications, 1980.

Huck, Gabe, ed. *Liturgy with Style and Grace: A Basic Manual for Planners and Ministers*. Rev. ed. Chicago: Liturgy Training Publications, 1984.

Keifer, Ralph. *To Give Thanks and Praise: General Instruction of the Roman Missal with Commentary for Musicians and Pastors*. Washington, D.C.: National Association of Pastoral Musicians, 1980.

Sheppard, Lancelot, ed. *The New Liturgy: A Comprehensive Introduction*. London: Longman & Todd, 1970.

Soubigou, Louis. *A Commentary on the Prefaces and the Eucharistic Prayers of the Roman Missal*. Trans. by John A. Otto. Collegeville, Minnesota: The Liturgical Press, 1971.

Walsh, Eugene, S.S. *Guidelines for Effective Worship*. Phoenix: North American Liturgy Resources, 1974.

Other Useful Resources on the Mass

Adam, Adolf. *The Liturgical Year.* New York: Pueblo Publishing Company, 1981.

Bishops' Committee on the Liturgy. *Environment and Art in Catholic Worship.* Washington, D.C.: USCC, 1978.

Bouley, Alan. *From Freedom to Formula.* Washington, D.C.: The Catholic University of America Press, 1981.

Champlin, Joseph. *The Mass in a World of Change.* Notre Dame: Ave Maria Press, 1973.

Coyle, Tom. *This Is Our Mass.* Mystic, Connecticut: Twenty-Third Publications, 1985.

Davies, J. G., ed. *The New Westminster Dictionary of Liturgy and Worship.* Philadelphia: The Westminster Press, 1986.

Deiss, Lucien. *The Mass.* Trans. by Lucien Deiss and Michael S. Driscoll. Collegeville, Minnesota: The Liturgical Press, 1992.

Dix, Gregory. *The Shape of the Liturgy.* London: Dacre Press, 1945.

Geaney, Denis J., O.S.A., and Dolly Sokol. *Parish Celebrations: A Reflective Guide for Liturgy Planning.* Mystic, Connecticut: Twenty-Third Publications, 1983.

Gusmer, Charles W. "Reviewing the Order of Mass." *Worship* 57, no. 4 (July 1983): 345-348.

Hovda, Robert. *Dry Bones.* Washington, D.C.: The Liturgical Press, 1973.

Huck, Gabe. *Preaching about the Mass.* Chicago: Liturgy Training Publications, 1992.

Jasper, R. C. D., and Cuming, G. J. *Prayers of the Eucharist Early & Reformed.* London: Collins Publishers, 1975.

Jungmann, Josef A. *The Mass: An Historical, Theological and Pastoral Survey.* Collegeville, Minnesota: The Liturgical Press, 1976.

———. *The Mass of the Roman Rite: Its Origins and Development (Missarum Sollemnia).* 2 vols. Trans. by Francis A. Brunner. New York: Benziger Brothers, Inc., 1951. One-volume edition revised and abridged by Charles K. Riepe, *The Mass of the Roman Rite.* Westminster, Maryland: Christian Classics, Inc., 1978.

Kavanagh, Aidan. *On Liturgical Theology.* New York: Pueblo Publishing Company, 1984.

———. *Elements of Rite: A Handbook of Liturgical Style.* New York: Pueblo Publishing Company, 1982.

Keifer, Ralph A. *Blessed and Broken: An Exploration of the Contemporary Experience of God in Eucharistic Celebration.* Wilmington, Delaware: Michael Glazier, Inc., 1982.

————. *Mass in Time of Doubt: The Meaning of the Mass for Catholics Today.* Washington, D.C.: National Association of Pastoral Musicians, 1983.

Klauser, Theodor. *A Short History of the Western Liturgy.* New York: Oxford University Press, 1979.

The Liturgy Documents: A Parish Resource. Chicago: Liturgy Training Publications, 1985.

Loret, Pierre. *The Story of the Mass: From the Last Supper to the Present Day.* Trans. by Dorothy Marie Zimmerman, S.S.N.D. Ligouri, Missouri: Ligouri Publications, 1982.

Martimort, A. G., ed. *The Church at Prayer.* Collegeville, Minnesota: The Liturgical Press, 1992.

————. *The Eucharist.* Collegeville, Minnesota: The Liturgical Press, 1986.

————. *Principles of the Liturgy.* Collegeville, Minnesota: The Liturgical Press, 1987.

McManus, Frederick R. "Genius of the Roman Rite Revisited." *Worship* 54, no. 4 (July 1980): 360-378.

Mitchell, Nathan. *Cult and Controversy: The Worship of the Eucharist Outside Mass.* New York: Pueblo Publishing Company, 1982.

Murphy Center for Liturgical Research, The. *Made, Not Born.* Notre Dame: University of Notre Dame Press, 1976.

Patino, J. *The New Order of Mass: Official Text of Instruction and Commentary.* Collegeville, Minnesota: The Liturgical Press, 1966.

Power, David. *Unsearchable Riches: The Symbolic Nature of Liturgy.* New York: Pueblo Publishing Company, 1984.

————. *The Sacrifice We Offer: The Tridentine Dogma and Its Reinterpretion.* New York: Crossroad, 1987.

————. *Gifts That Differ: Lay Ministries Established and Unestablished.* New York: Pueblo Publishing Company, 1980.

Roguet, A. M. *The New Mass.* Trans. by Walter van de Putte. New York: Catholic Book Publishing Company, 1970.

Searle, Mark. *Liturgy Made Simple.* Collegeville, Minnesota: The Liturgical Press, 1981.

Searle, Mark, ed. *Sunday Morning: A Time for Worship.* Collegeville, Minnesota: The Liturgical Press, 1982.

Seasoltz, R. Kevin. *Living Bread, Saving Cup.* Collegeville, Minnesota: The Liturgical Press, 1982.

Smits, Kenneth, O.F.M. Cap. "A Congregational Order of Worship." *Worship* 54, no. 1 (January 1980): 55-75.

Taft, Robert. *Beyond East and West: Problems in Liturgical Understanding.* Washington, D.C.: The Pastoral Press, 1984.

Talley, Thomas J. *The Origins of the Liturgical Year.* New York: Pueblo Publishing Company, 1986.

Untener, Kenneth E. *Sunday Liturgy Can Be Better.* Cincinnati: St. Anthony Messenger Press, 1980.

Walsh, Eugene A., S.S. *Parish Mass Planning: A Summary of Priorities.* Old Hickory, Tennessee: Pastoral Arts Associates of North America, 1981.

———. *Practical Suggestions for Celebrating Sunday Mass.* Glendale, Arizona: Pastoral Arts Associates of North America, 1978.

———. *The Ministry of the Celebrating Community.* Glendale, Arizona: Pastoral Arts Associates of North America, 1977.

———. *The Order of Mass: Guidelines.* Glendale, Arizona: Pastoral Arts Associates of North America, 1979.

———. *The Theology of Celebration.* Glendale, Arizona: Pastoral Arts Associates of North America, 1977.

Resources for Planning

Dallen, James. *Liturgical Celebration: Possible Patterns.* 3 vols. Phoenix: North American Liturgy Resources, 1973-1975.

Grail of England. *Themes, Prayers, Intercessions.* 3 vols. Cincinnati: World Library Publications, 1971-1973.

Irwin, Kevin. *Celebrant's Guide to the Sacramentary.* 3 vols. New York: Pueblo Publishing Company, 1975-1977. Revised edition, *Sunday Worship: A Planning Guide to Celebration.* New York: Pueblo Publishing Company, 1983.

Jarrell, Stephen T. *Guide to the Sacramentary for Sundays and Festivals.* Chicago: Liturgy Training Publications, 1983.

Marchal, Michael. *Adapting the Liturgy: Creative Ideas for the Church Year.* San Jose, California: Resource Publications, Inc., 1989.

Mazziotta, Richard, C.S.C. *We Pray to the Lord: General Intercessions Based on the Scriptural Readings for Sundays and Holy Days.* Notre Dame: Ave Maria Press, 1984.

Nocent, Adrian, O.S.B. *The Liturgical Year.* 4 vols. Trans. by Matthew J. O'Connell. Collegeville, Minnesota: The Liturgical Press, 1978.

Prayers of the Faithful: Cycles A, B, C. New York: Pueblo Publishing Company, 1977.

Ryan, G. Thomas, Mary Beth Kunde-Anderson, Timothy Fitzgerald, and Peter Scagnelli. *Sourcebook for Sundays and Seasons*. Chicago: Liturgy Training Publications, published annually.

Tuzik, Robert L. *Christ Living Among His People: A Guide to Understanding and Celebrating the Liturgical Year*. Washington, D.C.: The Federation of Diocesan Liturgical Commissions, 1984.

Zappulla, Robert, et al. *Modern Liturgy Planning Guide*. San Jose, California: Resource Publications, Inc., 1987.

Resources for Presiders

Fleming, Austin. *Yours is a Share: The Call of Liturgical Ministry*. Washington, D.C.: The Pastoral Press, 1985.

Hovda, Robert W. "For Presiders/Preachers." In *Touchstones for Liturgical Ministers*. Ed. by Virginia Sloyan. Washington, D.C.: The Liturgical Conference and the Federation of Diocesan Liturgical Commissions, 1978.

―――. *Strong, Loving and Wise: Presiding in Liturgy*. Rev. ed. Washington, D.C.: The Liturgical Conference, 1981.

Simons, George F. *Faces and Facets: A Workbook for the Liturgical Celebrant*. Chicago: Life in Christ, a Division of ACTA, 1977.

Resources for Deacons

Hovda, Robert W. "For Deacons." In *Touchstones for Liturgical Ministers*. Ed. by Virginia Sloyan. Washington, D.C.: The Liturgical Conference and the Federation of Diocesan Liturgical Commissions, 1987.

Kwatera, Michael, O.S.B. *The Liturgical Ministry of the Deacon*. Collegeville, Minnesota: The Liturgical Press, 1985.

Resources for Acolytes

Guentert, Kenneth. *Young Server's Book of the Mass*. San Jose, California: Resource Publications, Inc., 1987.

Hovda, Robert W. *There Are Different Ministries*. Washington, D.C.: The Liturgical Conference, 1975.

Kwatera, Michael, O.S.B. *The Ministry of Servers*. Collegeville, Minnesota: The Liturgical Press, 1982.

Lanz, Kerry J. *The Complete Server*. Wilton, Connecticut: Morehouse-Barlow, 1978.

Nevins, Albert J., M.M. *Called to Serve: A Guidebook for Altar Servers*. Huntington, Indiana: Our Sunday Visitor, Inc., 1981.

Ryan, G. Thomas. "For Acolytes." In *Touchstones for Liturgical Ministers*. Ed. by Virginia Sloyan. Washington, D.C.: The Liturgical Conference and the Federation of Diocesan Liturgical Commissions, 1978.

Resources for Readers

Allen, Horace T., Jr., ed. *The Reader as Minister*. Washington, D.C.: The Liturgical Conference, 1980.

Carr, William M. *A Handbook for Lectors*. Ramsey, New Jersey: Paulist Press, 1968.

Champlin, Joseph M. *Messengers of God's Word: A Handbook for Lectors*. Ramsey, New Jersey: Paulist Press, 1982.

DuCharme, Jerry and Gail. *Lector Becomes Proclaimer*. San Jose, California: Resource Publications, Inc., 1985. *Workbook Edition*, 1989.

Fleming, Austin. *Yours is a Share: The Call of Liturgical Ministry*. Washington, D.C.: The Pastoral Press, 1985.

Hardman, Benedict E. *Speech and Oral Reading Techniques for Mass Lectors and Commentators*. Collegeville, Minnesota: The Liturgical Press, 1966.

Harrison, J. B. *Proclaiming His Word*. New York: Pueblo Publishing Company, 1973.

Lee, Charlotte. *Oral Reading of the Scriptures*. Boston: Houghton-Mifflin Company, 1974.

Lonergan, Ray. *A Well-Trained Tongue: Workbook for Proclaimers*. Chicago: Liturgy Training Publications, 1982.

Sloyan, Gerard S. "For Readers." In *Touchstones for Liturgical Ministers*. Ed. by Virginia Sloyan. Washington, D.C.: The Liturgical Conference and the Federation of Diocesan Liturgical Commissions, 1978.

Staudacher, Joseph M. *Laymen Proclaim the Word*. Chicago: Franciscan Herald Press, 1973.

Tate, Judith. *Manual for Lectors*. Dayton: Pflaum Publishing Company, 1975.

Wallace, James A. *The Ministry of Lectors*. Collegeville, Minnesota: The Liturgical Press, 1981.

Workbook for Lectors and Gospel Readers. Notes by Aelred Rosser, OSB. Chicago: Liturgy Training Publications, published annually.

Resources for Communion Ministers

Belford, William J. *Special Ministers of the Eucharist.* New York: Pueblo Publishing Company, 1979.

Champlin, Joseph P. *An Important Office of Immense Love.* New York: Paulist Press, 1979.

Fleming, Austin. *Yours is a Share: The Call of Liturgical Ministry.* Washington, D.C.: The Pastoral Press, 1985.

Hovda, Robert W. *There Are Different Ministries.* Washington, D.C.: The Liturgical Conference, 1975.

Huck, Gabe. *The Communion Rite at Sunday Mass.* Chicago: Liturgy Training Publications, 1989.

Kay, Melissa. "For Ministers of Communion." In *Touchstones for Liturgical Ministers.* Ed. by Virginia Sloyan. Washington, D.C.: The Liturgical Conference and the Federation of Diocesan Liturgical Commissions, 1978.

Kwatera, Michael, O.S.B. *The Ministry of Communion.* Collegeville, Minnesota: The Liturgical Press, 1983.

Resources for Pastoral Musicians

Bauman, William A. *The Ministry of Music: A Guide for the Practicing Church Musician.* 2nd edition. Ed. by Elaine Rendler and Thomas Fuller. Washington, D.C.: The Liturgical Conference, 1979.

Bishops' Committee on the Liturgy. *Church Music Today.* Washington, D.C.: USCC, 1982.

Braun, H. Myron. *What Every Choir Member Should Know.* Old Hickory, Tennessee: Pastoral Arts Associates of North America, 1982.

Christian Music Directories: Printed Music. San Jose, California: Resource Publications, Inc., updated annually.

Christian Music Directories: Recorded Music. San Jose, California: Resource Publications, Inc., updated annually.

Connolly, Michael. *The Parish Cantor: Helping Catholics Pray in Song.* Old Hickory, Tennessee: Pastoral Arts Associates of North America, 1981.

Fleming, Austin. *Yours is a Share: The Call of Liturgical Ministry.* Washington, D.C.: The Pastoral Press, 1985.

Hansen, James. *The Ministry of the Cantor.* Collegeville, Minnesota: The Liturgical Press, 1984.

Hartgen, William J. "For Musicians." In *Touchstones for Liturgical Ministers.* Ed. by Virginia Sloyan. Washington, D.C.: The Liturgical Conference and the Federation of Diocesan Liturgical Commissions, 1978.

Huck, Gabe. *How Can I Keep from Singing? Thoughts about Liturgy for Musicians.* Chicago: Liturgy Training Publications, 1989.

Johnson, Lawrence J. *The Ministers of Music.* Washington, D.C.: National Association of Pastoral Musicians, 1983.

Kern, Jan. *Eighty-Six Prefaces from the Roman Missal.* Chicago: GIA Publications, 1973.

McKenna, Edward J. *The Ministry of Musicians.* Collegeville, Minnesota: The Liturgical Press, 1983.

Middlecamp, Ralph. *Introduction to Catholic Music Ministry.* Glendale, Arizona: Pastoral Arts Associates of North America, 1978.

Patterson, Keith L. *Evaluating Your Liturgical Music Ministry.* San Jose, California, 1993.

Sotak, Diana Kodner. *Handbook for Cantors.* Chicago: Liturgy Training Publications, 1988.

Winter, Miriam Therese. *Why Sing? Toward a Theology of Catholic Church Music.* Washington, D.C.: National Association of Pastoral Musicians, 1984.

Resources for Ministers of Hospitality

Fleming, Austin. *Yours is a Share: The Call of Liturgical Ministry.* Washington, D.C.: The Pastoral Press, 1985.

Hovda, Robert. *There Are Different Ministries.* Washington, D.C.: The Liturgical Conference, 1975.

Smith, Gregory F., O.Carm. *The Ministry of Ushers.* Collegeville, Minnesota: The Liturgical Press, 1981.

Young, Elizabeth. "For Ushers." In *Touchstones for Liturgical Ministers.* Ed. by Virginia Sloyan. Washington, D.C.: The Liturgical Conference and the Federation of Diocesan Liturgical Commissions, 1978.

Resources for Creators of the Environment

Gurak, Eileen. *Using Art in Sunday Worship.* San Jose, California: Resource Publications, Inc., 1990.

Lokken, James A. "For Environment and Audio-Visuals." In *Touchstones for Liturgical Ministers.* Ed. by Virginia Sloyan. Washington, D.C.: The Liturgical Conference and the Federation of Diocesan Liturgical Commissions, 1978.

Simons, Thomas G., and James M. Fitzpatrick. *The Ministry of Liturgical Environment.* Collegeville, Minnesota: The Liturgical Press, 1984.

Periodicals

Assembly (formerly *Hucusque*). Newsletter issued by the Notre Dame Center for Pastoral Liturgy, P.O. Box 81, Notre Dame, Indiana 46556.

Church. Published four times a year for members by the National Pastoral Life Center. Editorial office is located at 299 Elizabeth Street, New York, New York 10012.

Hosanna. A publication of WinterSun Inc., an affiliation of North American Liturgy Publications. Bimonthly. 10802 N. 23rd Avenue, Phoenix, Arizona 85029.

Liturgy. An ecumenical journal containing articles on liturgy, ritual, and prayer. Each issue is devoted to a particular theme. Issued quarterly. The Liturgical Conference, 8750 Georgia Avenue, Suite 123, Silver Spring, Maryland 20910.

Liturgy 90. Short articles, questions and answers, notices of workshops and programs. Eight issues a year. Liturgy Training Publications, 1800 N. Hermitage, Chicago, Illinois 60622-1101.

Modern Liturgy. Each issue focuses on practical advice for the various members of the parish team. Published ten times a year. Resource Publications, Inc., 160 E. Virginia Street, #290, San Jose, California 95112-5876.

National Bulletin on Liturgy. A review published five times a year by the Canadian Conference of Catholic Bishops. Each issue deals with a specific subject. Publications Service, 90 Parent Avenue, Ottawa, Ontario K1N 7B1, Canada.

Newsletter: Bishops' Committee on the Liturgy. Newsletter containing information on liturgical revisions, Vatican decisions, policies, etc. Issued monthly. Bishops' Committee on the Liturgy, 1312 Massachusetts Avenue, N.W., Washington, D.C. 20005.

Pastoral Music. A bimonthly publication of the National Association of Pastoral Musicians. Issued to members as part of membership dues. Also available to non-members. National Association of Pastoral Musicians, 225 Sheridan Street, N.W., Washington, D.C. 20011.

Today's Parish. Published bimonthly. Frequently contains articles on liturgical celebration. Twenty-Third Publications, P.O. Box 180, West Mystic, Connecticut 06388.

Worship. A bimonthly journal devoted to substantive issues in liturgy and sacramental theology. Collegeville, Minnesota 56321.

Useful Addresses

ACTA. 1045 Columbian Avenue, Oak Park, Illinois 60302.

Alba House. 2187 Victory Boulevard, Staten Island, New York 10314.

American Catholic Press. 1224 Rossell Avenue, Oak Park, Illinois 60302.

Ave Maria Press. Notre Dame, Indiana 46556.

Bishops' Committee on the Liturgy. 1312 Massachusetts Avenue, N.W., Washington, D.C. 20005.

Catholic Book Publishing Company. 257 W. 17th Street, New York, New York 10011.

Christian Classics. P.O. Box 30, Westminster, Maryland 21157.

Federation of Diocesan Liturgical Commissions. P.O. Box 29039, Washington, D.C. 20017.

Franciscan Herald Press. 1434 W. 51st Street, Chicago, Illinois 60609.

GIA Publications, Inc. 7404 S. Mason Avenue, Chicago, Illinois 60609.

Houghton-Mifflin. 2 Park Street, Boston, Massachusetts 02107.

J.S. Paluch Company, Inc. 3825 N. Willow Road, P.O. Box 2703, Schiller Park, Illinois 60176.

Ligouri Publications. One Ligouri Drive, Ligouri, Missouri 63057.

Liturgy Training Publications. 1800 N. Hermitage, Chicago, Illinois 60622.

Morehouse-Barlow Company. 78 Danbury Road, Wilton, Connecticut 16897.

National Association of Pastoral Musicians. 225 Sheridan Street, N.W., Washington, D.C. 20011.

North American Liturgy Resources. 10802 N. 23rd Avenue, Phoenix, Arizona 85029.

Our Sunday Visitor, Inc. 200 Noll Plaza, Huntington, Indiana 46705.

Pastoral Arts Associates of North America. 4201 Old Hickory Boulevard, Old Hickory, Tennessee 37138.

Paulist Press. 545 Island Road, Ramsey, New Jersey 07446.

Pflaum/Cebco. 2285 Arbor Boulevard, Dayton, Ohio 45439.

Pueblo Publishing Company, Inc. 1860 Broadway, New York, New York 10023.

Resource Publications, Inc. 160 E. Virginia Street, #290, San Jose, California 95112-5876.

St. Anthony Messenger Press. 1615 Republic Street, Cincinnati, Ohio 45210.

The Liturgical Conference. 8750 Georgia Avenue, Suite 123, Silver Spring, Maryland 20910-3621.

The Liturgical Press. Collegeville, Minnesota 56321.

The Pastoral Press. 225 Sheridan Street, N.W., Washington, D.C. 20011.

Twenty-Third Publications. P.O. Box 180, Mystic, Connecticut 06355.

University of Notre Dame Press. Notre Dame, Indiana 46556.

USCC Publications Office. 3211 Fourth Street, N.E. Washington, D.C. 20017.

World Library Publications, Inc. 3815 N. Willow Road, P.O. Box 2005, Schiller Park, Illinois 60176.